THE CHILDREN OF THE COUNTERCULTURE

THE CHILDREN OF THE COUNTER-CULTURE

JOHN ROTHCHILD
and
SUSAN BERNS WOLF

Doubleday & Company, Inc.
Garden City, New York
1976

For
Margie and Michael

Introduction

Old Jerry Rubin, remembered for saying "kill your parents" in the 1960s, had thought of writing a book called *Eating My Words* for the 1970s. He is not a father, so the retraction would not benefit him directly; but a lot of the people who used his slogan to express their mood in the 1960s are now on the other side of the parental fence. Abbie Hoffman might appreciate the retraction, he has a kid; some of the Weathermen have kids; the commune pioneers have kids; the acid freaks and Jesus freaks and all the people you used to see hitchhiking around New Mexico and living in caves are now doing it with children at their sides. It is a strange notion at first, that of counterculture parents, for the very thing that unites the amorphous collection of people in our minds is that they did things to horrify their own parents. We have frozen them in time, really, their time of adolescent rebellion. But the people who once made news every time they gave somebody the finger have now gone off and had their babies in anonymous corners of America. As parents, they have become private citizens. And some of the children of the new culture are now six, seven, eight years old.

Where had they gone, all those judge-taunters and war-busters and parent-worriers and armies of the night? It is somewhat ironic how the counterculture dropped off the back pages of the newspaper just as the front page began to print verifications of what once were called paranoid hippie fantasies. Government bugging, the telephone company spying, the corruption of megacorporations, cheating in the Soap Box Derby, VD in the Girl Scouts, the dissolution of the family, couples fighting *not* to take custody of the children after divorce, the whole weird, crumbling country you read about in the *East Village Other* or The Fabulous Furry Freak Brothers comic books, you can now read about in *Time,* or hear about at Rotary Club lunches. They were the first to inform us we were in terrible trouble, those hippies and flower children, and now that the rest of the country is oozing with disbelief, the original finger-pointers have disappeared. No longer protesting and making noise. That's one of the things that motivated Susan and me to write this book—we had enough contact with 1960s people to know they were still out there somewhere and that they had not become insurance salesmen in Kansas City. The fact that they were no longer making public trouble made us suspect that the people who were first with the protests might be first with some new answers. About how to raise children. About how to get out of the endless cycle the rest of us are in—selling each other inedible hamburgers and bad news.

During the 1960s, all the protests and challenges to the regular American way of life were not taken seriously by the majority of Americans—and childhood itself had a lot to do with that. The hippie hegiras and lifestyle changes were carried out by children, many still getting allowances, children who did not have to interrupt their acid trips to feed babies. All those struggles for self-worth were so much a part of the growing pains of a specific generation of young people that they could be ignored as elaborate puberty rites. I couldn't see that then, being part of the generation that protested, but I could see it now. Susan had two children, Chauncey (five) and Bernsie (three), and she was wondering what to do with her life and theirs.

I don't think she would have learned anything from a Haight-Ashbury groupie in the late 1960s. But we found we had a lot to learn from commune parents who have kept up their new life with children at their sides. There are thousands of people in America who have escaped the work trap and the consumer trap, and they have managed to do it with children. But what about the children? It is the question at which many people who consider dumping their careers or jobs or marriages inevitably pull back. We wanted to discover what had happened to the children of dropouts and Weathermen and commune pioneers who had not pulled back.

Our first contact with counterculture children was in Miami, where Susan and I and Chauncey and Bernsie were living. The odds against any real hippies wanting to be in Miami were so great, we thought, that if we found even one here, then there would be thousands elsewhere around the country. There turned out to be dozens of people living at the Maya House, a sort of Volkswagen bus stop for people on their way up and down the commune trail from Bolivia to California. An old Spanish stucco house, with constant rock music blaring from the balcony, painted busses choking the driveway, old sleeping bags drip-drying in the trees. The people were either naked or dressed in elaborate orange kaftans and gauzy guru robes. They spent most of the day hugging each other in a giant rugby scrum of affection, swaying in a silent, stoned buzz like so many plants. When one of them moved from the scrum (which was not often) it was usually to bend down and pick up a grapefruit off the ground—fallen fruit appeared to be their only visible means of support.

A garden of love it was, right out of the flower children, except that these people were in their late twenties and thirties and kept swaying in spite of the little children that ran around and between them. The children at Maya treated this collective lump of parenthood as if it were a sand dune. Even before we got to know the children, Susan was amazed at the mothers. Amazed because Susan herself had once taken a lot of psychedelics—she recognized the stoned, euphoric state—and had given them up because she decided it was impossible to be stoned and also to be

3

a mother. Too many worries and fears about the children intervened. But these Maya parents, whoever they were, had carried their flowers and that carefree buzz in their heads right into parenthood.

We got to know one of the families, on its way to North Carolina to start an organic vegetable farm. The man's name was Billy, somewhere in his middle twenties, and he wore leather Davy Crockett clothes and a black patch over one eye. Billy was the musician for the scrum; he sat cross-legged on a blanket and every ten minutes or so would plunk a single note on his guitar, and one of the scrum people would turn around, smile at him, and say, "Far out." He said he was staying at Maya House until he got a part for his truck. (There were always several people at these nomadic communes waiting for parts.) Billy had just fallen in love with Lisa, a woman in her early thirties who wore her blond hair long and uncombed to her waist, the perfect vision of a nymph. Lisa told us she had done "all the trips"—meaning that she had lived in communes, traveled to Colombia on mystical treks, gone to California for tribal gatherings, and now she was heading for North Carolina to start a farm with Billy. She had two adorable children, Hector (four) and Treemonisha (five), who spent the day at Maya running around in clean but faded Pakistani shirts. We asked Lisa a lot of questions, to which she had no answers: where the trip would take her, where the farm was located, if the farm could be paid off, where the money would come from, if she and Billy would stay together, where the part for the truck could be found, where the children would go to school, how the children accepted being schlepped around the country, who was preparing dinner for that night. Lisa didn't seem to care about any of this. She kept talking about universal love and how friends always help out and how things always get together. The more questions we asked, the closer she sat to us, until finally she began rubbing strawberry perfume on our necks and faces and massaging our shoulders to calm us down. We were being reporters; she was treating us as two totally demented paranoids who needed to be tranquilized.

It was impossible for us not to measure our own situation

against that of Billy and Lisa. From the outside, it looked the same—two battered Volkswagens about to leave on a trek across the country, with a man and a woman who were not married and two young children in each car. Susan and I were roughly the same age as Billy and Lisa, our children roughly the same age as theirs, and we wanted to jump into this project as fellow hippie travelers on the counterculture trail. That fantasy was hard to sustain, though, on closer inspection of how we were traveling. Our car was filled with rock-bottom necessities, carefully gleaned from a much larger pile of things we could have taken. There were two boxes of books for the children, and two boxes of toys and road games to keep them occupied. Four sleeping bags, a tent, a few pots and pans, five suitcases of clothes, plenty of maps, and of course an American Express card and a contract from Doubleday. This, as far as we were concerned, was hippie baggage. Not nearly enough to cover us in all emergencies, or to stop Susan from worrying about what might happen if the car broke down, or all the things we asked Lisa if she worried about. Susan's worries centered entirely on Chauncey and Bernsie.

Billy's car was totally empty except for a paper bag full of clothes and a few loose oranges and a guitar and a bottle to pee in. It was our first real understanding of the counterculture as the absence of something. What they had learned to do without, what they had chosen to do without. Neither Billy nor Lisa had a job, an income, a map, a credit card, a spare tire, or a sense of the future. Compared to them, we were covered on all flanks like Winnebago people, and yet there was no doubt which Volkswagen was more serene. Lisa and Billy exuded serenity, and even their children, Hector and Tree, were a lot less squirmy and whiny than Chauncey and Berns.

We wanted to follow Lisa and Billy and their children, and after a couple of days of getting massaged and hearing Lisa tell us that everything works out, their Volkswagen was fixed. They got in with their bag and their oranges and their little bottle, we got into our Coleman-loaded, game-fortified portable suburb and followed them. We wanted to get to know their children better, and we wanted to find out how they could live in such euphoric nonchalance. Secretly we thought they would never make North Carolina.

Unfortunately, we lost our chance to find out. Two hours up the turnpike, Bernsie said she had to pee and Chauncey wanted a drink, and both of them recognized the Howard Johnson's sign. Hector and Tree probably didn't know what Howard Johnson's was, Susan wasn't prepared to make Bernsie pee in her pants for the sake of our book, and we didn't carry an empty bottle. Chauncey would not have understood our denying him a cold drink—for five years he had gotten pretty much what he wanted. So we pulled into the exit, and I honked to warn Billy and Lisa that we were dropping off. But they just kept going. From our portable suburb, we watched the paper bag family disappear down the road. They had not given us a map to their farm, since nomadic hippies do not believe in maps, and they had shaken our tail at the first HoJo's.

We returned to Miami, with two hours to consider why this happened. Chauncey and Bernsie, by this time, were engaged in constant bickering over the toys we had bought to keep them quiet. We realized that our own attitude as parents had been the barrier between us and the Maya House nomads. Billy and Lisa, from what we had seen in their car, did not believe in padding their children's lives with toys or in making special pee stops for the sake of children. Whatever consequences their beliefs may have had on Tree and Hector, we could already see the consequences of our more traditional attitudes about children's rights. Chauncey and Bernsie were not supposed to be characters in this book; they were going along for the ride while Susan and I did interviews and took notes. But they kept getting into it. The HoJo incident was the first—and most trivial—of several months of challenges in which we tried to judge the children of a new lifestyle and ended up revealing our deficiencies as a family. Chauncey and Bernsie often blew our cover. It was impossible to be circumspect and reportorial about certain commune children when we could see so clearly that their children were better behaved than ours. We tried to be noncommittal observers of counterculture life, but it was difficult not to be swayed when

Bernsie was the only petulant whiner among a group of forty children, or when Chauncey interrupted a group project to count his quarters. One thing we quickly learned is that all those stages that Dr. Spock calls natural are not natural at all. After meeting a lot of quiet, well-mannered two-year-olds, we had to admit that we *taught* Bernsie the Terrible Twos.

There might have been a time when a smug, solid nuclear family could have gone out to judge the counterculture and come back smugger and solider. Maybe a family like that still exists. But the experiences of visiting several dozen communes and radical homes had the reverse effect on Susan and me. We left Miami as two progressive, aware parents who had each once been married and didn't have to do that anymore, who were raising Chauncey and Bernsie in a much more open and aware manner than our parents had raised us. We certainly didn't expect to learn anything from the alternative people we wanted to visit—we already let Chauncey and Bernsie puff on the joints being passed around and we already had to warn them not to say "motherfucker" at Disneyland. And we couldn't think of a more radical thing than that.

Where does the counterculture begin for a child? With his first joint, with being allowed to admit he farted, with seeing his parents make love, with having a dropout for a father, with having no father at all, with a girl who wears football pads, with no television, or with something more drastic, like growing up in a cave? So many people have adopted the notion "alternative" to describe their lives that we knew we could not cover them all. The false start with the nomad family had taught us that we could not begin so ambitiously. We would meet other nomads later down the road, but we decided to start our investigation with the people around us. People who still lived in cities but sent their children to free schools. People who call themselves radical but still put up with straight neighbors. Susan and I were in that category, and we knew lots of other families like that from Chauncey's free school. Children who were being taken on slight detours from the regular American program, who were not being prepared for careers, who were not being raised on Victorian sexual taboos and fear of drugs. Children who still live in cities and have to learn the double standard—when to be cool and when not to be cool.

We started with the free families still in touch with America, and moved out from there—through the political radicals who live in nuclear families; through the urban communes; rural communes; a whole network of rural communes that has become a kind of civilization; isolated new religious communities like the Hare Krishnas; through a behavior modification center called Synanon; and finally to Stephen Gaskin's Farm, where the children are as alien to regular America as Red Chinese children would be. This book does not attempt to be comprehensive and it does not attempt to be academic. It is the journey of one family through the small cracks in the American identity and outward into uncharted territory. Always with our eyes on the children.

There are more counterculture people out there than you might think. Communes are thriving to a far greater degree than we had imagined—we had to settle on one example of each type of commune and then write about that. Communes are not heavily publicized, of course—we could arrive in an area like New Mexico or Arkansas, stop in at one place, and learn of several others hidden in the nearby mountains. People hanging out at the edge of civilization, with their own wind generators and water supply and separate food system, independent of the world markets, prepared for whatever happens. Children abound in communes as they did in old-time rural farm families, and having them is not viewed with suspicion. We calculated that with several hundred communes and an average of ten children in each, the second generation will outnumber many of the larger Indian tribes in America.

It is hard to generalize about the various groups that we lived with for several months, for they have all gone in such different directions. But they did come mostly from the same place. White, college-educated Americans. Even in the austere, dirt-scratching survival communes, most of the inhabitants were ex-professors or people with degrees. Rarely did we see a black or a

Chicano. The children of the counterculture are children of people who were expected to become doctors or lawyers, people who grew up in middle-class America and then rejected it. Maybe they were still supported by middle-class America during the rebellions of the 1960s. But not any more. The commune parents have been surviving on their wits for several years.

It is also hard to generalize about the children, except to say that most of them are between three and eight years old. But we did discover one surprising thing. From our perspective in Miami, we envisioned that the weirdest, most untamed children would be found in isolated Western communes. I worried about those naked, acid-crazed Easy Rider kids sneaking up on us and burning down our tent. As it turned out, the most outrageous and tormented children, the most hostile children we saw were the three children from the Miami free families. It was in the isolated communes, at the far fringes of America, that we discovered the best-behaved, most responsible children we had ever seen. Children so beyond our own experience that we could not even have fantasized their existence. Chauncey and Bernsie, by comparison, became the untamed savages—we realized that our vision of little tent-burners had more to do with regular Miami kids than the kids of Colorado communes.

While we began the book with the suspicion that a hippie child is a wild child, we ended up believing that well-behaved children are the most radical alternative to American society. The farther away from regular families and cities and careers that we get, the less obnoxious and self-centered the kids get. Which says something about the regular American family, and is the challenge of commune life to us.

1

The Free People

Nemo and Ellie are immediately recognizable as hip people. He and his ersatz Afro haircut (which might look better if he were black) and his frequently extended middle finger—Nemo's political body language. She and her see-through obscene tee shirts, where you aren't sure whether to pay attention to the printed pornography or the two real breasts. Together, Nemo and Ellie make an immediate statement on authority, sexuality, and politics that is vintage Columbia student revolt, Haight-Ashbury, Woodstock, Chicago Seven, Merry Pranksters. They wear the counterculture. Except for their faces, which have aged a little beyond the trustworthy age of thirty, they are carrying the youth rebellion into their middle years.

When Nemo and Ellie talk, separately or together, it always sounds like an editorial board meeting at the Great Speckled Bird. Not just in the filler words that even Walter Cronkite uses now, the "far-outs" and "groovies" and "rip-off" and "don't lay that trip on me, man," but in the entire content of their language, which revolves around the concepts of freedom and being uptight. Their life is a constant struggle for freedom. Against the uptight policeman who won't let them sit naked in the park. Against the uptight people who won't let them smoke dope. Against uptight schools and uptight people who have jobs and uptight parents who lay trips on their kids. They project an image of primitive euphoria—just floating through life, fucking without jealousy, surviving without work, bringing up a child without the use of that ugly word "don't." They make it seem so easy, as if their lives are one privileged hamlet where the revolution succeeded. All around them is the troubled and repressive regular American world.

Of course, they want to bring up their ten-year-old son, Ben, inside the privileged hamlet, to spare him all the rebellion that they and a generation around them faced in the 1960s. To go along with their new ethic, they have placed Ben in a free school, another part of the privileged hamlet. We knew about Ben because Chauncey was going to this same school. Susan and I were part of a group of parents who in one way or another agreed with Nemo and Ellie that regular schools are prisons, that Americans strangle their children with rules and routines and expectations, that a new generation of children should be raised more on Abbie Hoffman, less on Dr. Spock. When the free school parents sent a delegation to view a public school, their report sounded like a Southern senator's speech after his visit to communist Poland.

Take a look at the people who started the Miami free school. It shows how broad the dissatisfaction with the American culture is becoming. There was a yoga mother who had been celibate for six years; her daughter was in the school to get away from the "carnivores." There were Ellie and Nemo, who wanted to free their son from the influence of "fascists and neo-Victorians." An Okie woman who wore baggy Hawaiian mu-mus and carried bubble soap to blow in traffic jams and other uptight situations sent her son to avoid "the Mickey Mouse of required gym shorts in public schools." A scientist and his wife thought their child would be happier in an unstructured environment. A dropout computer programmer who lived on a boat wanted to spare his daughter from "the buzz saw of public education."

For these diverse families, choosing a free school seemed like an incredible step on many levels. For one thing, the school was not certified by the local authorities, it didn't have the required number of sinks and toilets, and was always in danger of being shut down. For another thing, the school kept making unannounced changes in location, moving around the neighborhood like a clandestine poker game, and you were never sure, when you drove your kid to the place, that it would still be there. And, most important, the educational vision of the free school began and ended with what was once called recess. There were no courses of any kind, no schedule, no grades, no permanent records, and no material to cover. The children spent the day milling around doing what they felt like doing—setting fires with large magnifying glasses, chasing each other on tricycles, building forts out of lawn chairs, trying (and mostly failing) to read comic books. The fear of stifling the children, of "laying a trip on them" was so great that education became the absence of teaching. The children were expected, like primitive man at the dawn of civilization, to discover the mysteries of life by accident, in their play. The theory was that the kids would set a fire and then come to the teacher, Dan, and say, "Hey, fire. How does it work?" But this assumed curiosity on the part of the children was a complete illusion—Dan would sit in the corner like an unused microscope while the children played on.

Whether or not this is a valid way to learn did not interest us particularly. It did not really interest any of the parents. They had put their children into the free school not for intellectual reasons, but for cultural ones. It was the whole American ethic of hard desks and pledges of allegiance and grades and perfect attendance and Thanksgiving turkeys that they wanted to bypass. It seemed, at first, like a severe, irrevocable choice between freedom and success. Chauncey was only five, so it didn't matter for him, but some of the children were nine and ten years old, and having them in this school meant they were falling behind in math and reading, losing ground in the competitive race toward college that now seems to begin in the first grade. A year or two in the free school, a year without records or folders of any kind, a year to learn not to value academic pressure and to reject authority, and who knows what would happen to these kids. The other parents, at the free school PTA meetings, said they understood the risks, but that their children's happiness was more important to them. They valued their children's freedom now more than their chance to get into Harvard later. An exact reversal of the sputnik age.

Susan and I couldn't quite believe it, the parents who still held down jobs and woke up to alarm clocks immersing their children in a totally unstructured world. We visited them in their houses, and we finally figured it out. They weren't really serious. The scientist couple, for instance, was glad to discuss this grave step they were taking with their son, Beano. They got a big kick from being interviewed about it, sitting in their living room, until we discovered that while they were getting the kick, Beano was doing his homework. Alone in his room. The subterfuge became apparent—they were cramming him by night so he could be free by day. They had him periodically tested to make sure he wasn't falling behind. They gave him a rigid schedule and plenty of discipline to counteract the free school playground. Beano's parents didn't admit it, but it was clear they still had very traditional expectations for him. They wanted him to spend his day in the new culture and still get into Harvard.

The dropout couple invited us onto their boat—their daughters Penny (eight) and Sue (six) had been in the free school from its beginning. The man, whose name was Pete, sat us down in the cabin and rolled us a joint and launched into a dramatic recounting of how he gave up on America and packed his family into a boat and headed south to become a drifter. During a precious lull in his monologue, we asked him if we could talk to the children about their problems in adjusting to their radical new lifestyle. No, he said, the kids were in the back room doing their homework. He also didn't like them around when he smoked grass.

Whatever might happen in other free schools around the country, most of the families in the Miami free school turned out to be like that. We spent several other evenings in traditional living rooms, with parents whose children ran wild by day and then were not allowed to bounce on the couch at night. The fantasy of the free school became obvious—it was a fantasy of anarchy which could be immediately abandoned at the first sign of trouble. The yoga mother, the boat family, the scientist family, and the mu-mu lady all ended this flirtation with freedom for their children after one year. The children were returned to the public school with no reported reentry problems. There was no reentry necessary, really, because, behind a kind of alternative posturing, the free school parents did not themselves lead free lives. That was the cause of the failure of this school. And it made us wary of the notion of alternative lifestyle; a person could be a dropout and still have a conventional relationship to his children, a person could be a woman's liberationist and still be a traditional authoritarian parent. We wanted to get away from lifestyles, and concentrate our investigation on children of parents who had changed their life content.

Taken to its limits, the free school concept was a scary one. A twenty-four-hour-a-day unstructured life is a hard one to accept for a child. Even with Chauncey, who was only five and was going to the school for fun, we didn't like the anarchic effect the school had on him. We had to do a lot of civilizing work in the afternoons to calm him down. It was understandable why parents who themselves still had jobs and schedules would draw back from the fantasy, just as they often drew back from the fantasy of open marriage at the first threat of an actual affair. There were three children, though, whose home lives did coincide with the philosophy of the free school. One of them was Ben, the son of Nemo and Ellie; the second was Nina, who happened to live down the street from us; and the third was LuAnne, who lived with her mother at the Maya House. All three of them were being raised on the premise that the other parents said they accepted—total freedom to do anything, no rules, no boundaries. They didn't have to go to bed. They didn't have to go to school. They were the glorious incarnations of the flower people.

Ben was known as the hippest kid in Miami. He was ten when we met him, a caricature that you could draw with your eyes closed—one earring, bead necklace instead of a shirt, long stringy blond hair, and an exposed rib cage associated with macrobiotic diets. He knew how to roll joints and do yoga exercises. There was a mystique about Ben—he was reputed to have made love to his mother when he was six years old, to have panhandled and scammed for his food on the docks of Colombia among the most sophisticated street urchins in the world, and to have spent only three months of his life in school. Ben didn't know how to read. In most places it would have been seen as a terrible disadvantage, but around Ben's parents and associates, his illiteracy was a kind of accomplishment. It meant that Ben was smart enough to escape truant officers, and it also meant that his brain hadn't been damaged by education. The prevailing view of public education was a lot of kids with chains wrapped around their heads like the Radio Free Europe ads.

At the free school, which is where we saw Ben, he was recognized as being different from the other children who already knew how to read and were sent here to liberate their spirits; Ben was by all accounts already free and was sent here to learn how to read. It seemed that Ben would have an easier time learning a basic skill than the other kids would have in approaching the image Ben already evoked as a product of Rousseau, Timothy Leary, Gauguin, Lord of the Flies, Jack Kerouac, the *East Village Other,* and Huckleberry Finn all rolled into one. He was a special child, a cosmic child who knew his place in the universe. "I'm a Sagittarius," he said, "a fire sign. My sun is rising in Scorpio." But he did not know the name of his real father.

Ben stood out from the other children. He looked leaner and tougher than the other city kids and he had a habit of staring at grownups in an accusatory way that made his eyes look like two sleepy Southern traffic cops. He had a way of answering questions with an indifference that resembled being hit in the chin by a shrug. An indifference that we took as a sure sign of a radical upbringing. He was beautiful with his blond hair and sunken eyes and hungry attitude. He didn't move like a WASP ("It must be his sexual experience"), he had the shuffling confidence of a Brazilian shoeshine boy. The girls at the school called him the "kissing bandit." The boys seemed to let him command the playground, even though he wasn't the biggest or even the oldest. The first day we watched him, he took all the available toys, blocks and chairs, and stacked them together into a gigantic fort, commandeering all the assets until none of the other thirty-five children had anything left to play with. Then he stood beside his fort calculating which children to let in and which to exile, and they all deferred to his will.

It was easy to match Ben up to his parents at the school's alternative PTA meeting. His father was Nemo the thirty-seven-year-old hippie anachronism. Nemo wasn't Ben's real father, but they had been together off and on for seven years and Ben called him "dad." Ellie, his mother, was an attractive woman in her late twenties who wore the see-through tee shirts. Nemo and Ellie don't tell you right away that they financed their counterculture life by working as a pimp-hooker team. It's not the moral aspects of the work that they're ashamed of; they don't like people to get the impression that they rely on a traditional job like that. Ellie says Ben was separated from her for virtually all of the first four years of his life, when she was off doing other things. (She doesn't say hooking.) "He was a little insecure after that," she said, "but now we are very together and will never be separated again, unless *he* wants to." Since those first years, Ben and Ellie and Nemo had moved from one side of the country to the other several times, passing through pacifism, macrobiotic cooking, yoga, Zen, Sufis, communes, encounter therapy, biofeedback, and Gurdjieff.

Ellie and Nemo were eager to talk about their son, the product of all these mantras and meditations; we had a long discussion with them in the back of their secondhand Mercedes-Benz while they drove to see the chiropractor. Nemo said Ben was different from regular American children because "he doesn't have trips laid onto him by uptight parents. It's amazing how many trips we can lay down." Ellie explained that Ben didn't have to brush his teeth ("They're his"), he had no bedtime hour, no specific dinner hour, no unpleasant chores to do, he could

17

sleep all day, smoke grass, stay out of school, even eat ice cream for breakfast. Wasn't there anything he couldn't do? "Well," Ellie said, "I don't like him to lay his trips on other people, especially if it is hurting or killing. Beyond that, nothing. I had a long talk with him and told him he can do what he wants, but just to come to me first so we could make our getaway if it's illegal."

"How does all this freedom affect him?" I wanted to know. "Ben can be himself at home," Ellie said. "Totally himself. He doesn't have to pretend. Outside of the house, he can *almost* be himself. He has to know who is cool and who isn't. A truant officer almost picked him up once, and now he watches out for them. If he isn't sure about somebody, he asks me. The other day some straight people came over, and Ben wanted to smoke a joint, but he came to me and whispered, 'Are they OK?' and I told him they weren't. He can mostly tell without asking."

"The thing about Ben," Nemo said, like he had been building up to this, "is like what I read the other day about fish tanks. If you put a baby shark in a fish tank it never grows beyond the size of a guppy, even though that little body has a potential shark inside it. A fish conforms to the size of the tank. So does a kid. Ben's tank isn't going to have walls, unless he puts them there."

Ben's tank is a seventy-five-thousand-dollar house with a large lawn and a lot of coconut and palm trees where Ellie and Nemo are hanging out rent-free. (Actually they are supposed to be paying the friend who loaned them the house, but they aren't.) Several people live there, including an astrologer named Sam who has just discovered his homosexuality, and his wife Patty, who is trying to work out her sexual problems, and has just discovered Ben. You can hardly enter the house without thinking of sex; like many houses that give away the obsessions of their inhabitants by a certain smell—pipe smoke, cooking oil, silver polish, antiseptic, perfume, grass—this house reeks of massage oil and incense. The living room is void of furniture, except for a piano; the house itself leads you toward the bedrooms like a carnival that somehow whisks you past the 4-H exhibits and onto the midway. The bedroom doors are open, people are drying

18

themselves from showers or giving each other massages, and since none of the grownups hold an outside job, the actual work of the house revolves around Sam's elaborate astrology charts, kneading, and group analysis. The first day we went to Ben's house a woman told us that Ellie was upstairs making it, and we could go up and watch or stay down and wait. We gravitated to the kitchen, the only place there were chairs, and waited.

From what Ellie told us that day, sex was a part of Ben's life in a way we had never encountered for a boy his age, and it was the basis on which she built the theory of his liberation. Not brushing your teeth and going to bed late was one thing, but Ellie considered Ben to be a superior child because he could get what was solidly out of reach of middle-class children, he wouldn't have to go through adolescence with the turned-down pages of *Tropic of Capricorn* because he already had the real thing. His mother. Ellie told us she had made love to him in a Mexico hotel when Ben was six years old. What does it mean to make love, for a little kid? "He had an intellectual orgasm," Ellie said, sitting there in the kitchen, and she said it with such solemnity that we forgot to laugh, we forgot she was talking about a kid of Chauncey's age who had a runny nose and collected bubble gum cards. Ellie saw letting Ben sleep with her as a symbolic act, a kind of primal jailbreak, so that she had freed him from a life of Freudian remorse and anguish that the rest of us go through. "I didn't like making it with him that much," she said. "I felt black and terrible. But it was good for Ben." Through this act of self-sacrifice, she had solved the Oedipal problem for Ben by letting him *win* it, by letting him conquer his mother, so "he would never have to be an atomic scientist and make bombs when he really wanted to get laid."

Ellie said Ben had already had many lovers. Patty, the woman who was breaking up with Sam and wore chokers and low-cut dresses and exuded so much sexuality that even her breathing was almost a promiscuous gesture, told us that Ben was irresistible. She liked to take showers with him and have him pour shaving cream all over her. She said at bedtime Ben had his choice between her or any number of other ladies who bragged of making it with him. "What if he wants to be by himself?" I asked. "Then he has to lock his door," she said.

Where was this spectacular child, whose radical training had wiped out the taboos of centuries, whose life flowed with simple primal rhythms, who was as spontaneous and natural as the Tasaday before they were introduced to Oreo cookies? Ben was in the driveway, tossing stones against the metal garage wall, looking bored. On the several occasions we visited him at home, he was always outside, always by himself. He said hello and attempted a smile, but it was the kind of smile that speeding motorists give to motorcycle cops: "I played your game, buster, now get off my back." It disappeared quickly into a sullen face. Ben looked as if he were always leaning against a telephone pole, even when he wasn't. He was also slightly uncommunicative, at least to strangers, and when asked why he didn't go to school all the time, he said, "I don't feel like it." When we changed the subject to something less personal, like astrology—"A lot of people talk about their signs," I said, "but I don't understand much about it"—Ben would snap back with answers like, "Well, why don't you go and ask *them*." And when we offered to do things for him, like teach him to play the guitar, he merely responded, "No deal." He approached us with a guardedness unlikely in a child who supposedly had escaped disappointments and repressive cruelty. That's how he looked, disappointed.

There were no playmates for Ben in this children's paradise where you could rifle the refrigerator and stay up and tell stories and throw pies on the floor. Children were around the neighborhood, they could be heard on the other side of the hedge. But except for Star, a six-year-old girl who lived with her mother in the garage apartment of Ben's house and infrequently hung out with Ben ("He's mean," she said), Ben didn't have friends. He said they were "around" but he seemed to exist in an adult world. Perhaps, we thought, he is too sophisticated for these other children; they want to jump rope, he wants to smoke dope.

Ben had plenty of time for us. We asked him what he liked to do. "Watch TV," he said. "Then why don't you?" "I don't have one." "Why not?" "My mother says it pollutes your mind." "Do you think she's right?" "I like it." So the one thing he wanted to do, he could not do. In all of his travels and experiences, he had picked up no hobbies, he didn't play cards or musical instruments, and he didn't know any magic tricks. He also lacked curiosity about learning any of these things, and since there was no order to his day, he had to rely on his own enthusiasm to get him through. His enthusiasm was limited for a ten-year-old boy you'd expect to be in the flush of discovery.

We began to think of Ben as a dull boy not to have made more of his privileged environment, until we paid attention to his environment. Nobody around him was doing anything, either. As a matter of fact, the toilet in the main house had been stopped up for months, and no one bothered to fix it. Ben was a younger version of their listlessness; he would sit on the lawn and then enter the house to eat a cookie or a sandwich (there were no regular mealtimes), hang around while grownups were talking, maybe take a few puffs on a joint, come back out again, ride his bicycle around the circle at the end of the block, and return. He spent a great deal of time looking for Nemo, asking where Nemo was, or calling through the house like a lost bird. Nemo either wasn't at home, or else he was busy in the bedroom. We actually never saw Ellie or Nemo together with Ben for more than five minutes at a time.

When Ellie explained about Ben's apparent lack of interest in the world, she said his head was in a spiritual place, that he liked to get high and uplevel himself in a way that couldn't be measured in stamp collections or report cards. Ellie mentioned a consciousness-raising course that she and Nemo and Ben had attended, a long session of sitting on the floor and looking people in the eye and spinning magic discs. "He was the only kid there," she said. "But he understood more than a lot of the grownups. He doesn't understand the words, but he gets the meaning." It sounded a little unbelievable, a kid sitting still for all those hours and feeding off psychic vibrations. Ben came into the room while we were talking. "Tell them how much you liked the course," Ellie said, and in one of those moments of revelation that mothers fear, Ben gave a most disinterested look and said, "It was OK." Ellie, not satisfied with his expression of commitment, took it farther: "There's another session next weekend, if you want to go." "I don't know," Ben said. "Well, you'll have to stay home alone then, Patty and Sam and Nemo are going." "Can I go over to Chauncey's and watch television?" he said. And we realized for the first time you don't have to be a conventional mother to have fantasies about your children; we had just seen the alternative version of the mother who brags about how much her kid likes piano lessons and then the boy interrupts to ask if he can miss the next one for a baseball game.

Ben still had sex to amuse him, of course; at least it seemed so from talking to the women about him. But we never saw him hang around the bedrooms or take a shower with Patty or exhibit the slightest interest in women. When people tried to talk to him about girls, he would give them a quizzical "What does that mean?" look.

Ben's relationship to sex became more understandable one day at the free school, when Nemo came to pick him up in the Mercedes. Nemo, who somehow managed to come off as the most concerned parent at the school meetings, liked to hang around the school during the afternoons. On this particular day, he motioned for one of the girls on the playground, an eight-year-old named Penny, to come over and talk to him. He was standing next to the fence, wearing blue Bermuda shorts and a Smoke Colombian tee shirt. He started up a conversation with this little girl, and she began to laugh, and Ben, who always wanted to know what his dad was doing, walked over to join the conversation. By this time, Nemo was talking loud enough to be heard all over the playground. "I was just telling your girlfriend that you couldn't be queer, because you ball chicks." Ben was completely taken aback: he started to fidget and look down as if he wished to be swallowed. "What do you mean?" he mumbled, as if to plead with Nemo to stop, but Nemo kept on, he was smiling and enjoying himself. "You know what I mean," he said to the growing crowd of free school kids. "What about the time with Margo in the sailboat?" The little girl smiled and somebody behind her called Ben "sex maniac," which was one of his school nicknames. Ben walked toward the car, on the verge of tears. "Why did you do that?" I asked Nemo. "I thought it was fun," he said. "Maybe I shouldn't have."

The real story came to life: this symbol of sexuality and free will was just a boy whose parents pushed his penis, pushed it and paraded it and discussed it the same way most parents push their children's minds and discuss their children's report cards. Sex was not the primal jailbreak for Ben, it was the only area where his parents hoped for his performance, where his exploits were important enough for Nemo to brag about—at Ben's expense—on the school playground. Put the pressure on the penis instead of on the mind, but you still have a pushy father. Ben's life at home began to make more sense, this boy who stayed outside while all the women waited for him inside; he was a sexual toy who could be dragged out like Tiberius' Little Minnows, the children employed for the emperor's pleasure. At school, Ben was embroiled in a conflict that most children don't face until puberty: he was aggressive and flirty, he did kiss the girls and make them cry, but they would call him "kissing bandit" and he would feel terrible and retreat into the solitude of the school office. It was not natural behavior for the playground, it was driven behavior.

It was interesting to watch Ben at the free school; he was one of the few children for whom the ethic of the school and the life of the home coincided. Most of the free school children came from relatively normal households, and the parents viewed the school as an antidote to their children's otherwise structured life. But for Ben, the school was an exact duplication of the formless days he spent at home, and there was nobody at the school who wanted to repress him by paying attention to him. You would think that Ben would be accustomed to this sort of scene, and yet of all the students in the unstructured school, Ben had the most trouble. He arrived late in the morning—if he came at all—parking his bicycle next to the fence and walking into an empty side room. He spent most of the day alone, struggling with comic books which he didn't know how to read. He neither asked for nor was he given formal lessons of any kind. He also shied away from group activities. Dan the teacher told us, "I tried, man. But you can't force a kid to learn if he doesn't want to. It'll have to come from him."

The image we had of Ben the first day he built the fort was quickly revised. The other children sometimes deferred to his wishes in a fearful way, but they uniformly told us they did not like him, and the other boys were fond of calling him the "chicken bully." Ben did usually manage to get into trouble during the day, which is not easy to do at a free school. He liked to take tricycles away from five-year-olds.

Ben was not always mean. He and Chauncey were quite friendly with each other, an unlikely liaison between a ten-year-old sophisticate and a five-year-old. Ben began to visit our house quite often to see Chauncey, to watch television, or to go to movies with us, something he rarely had a chance to do at home. We didn't mind him being with Chauncey, other than to wonder about his emotional maturity for wanting to, but Ben was difficult to deal with. He had a habit of taking things one step too far, an extra pull that would rip the page of the book he was looking at, one too many chairs overturned, a playful slap that was hard enough to be suspect, a shoving match that was a little too persistent. He always managed to do just enough to get grownups angry at him. If asked to stop doing something, he would give one of his fuck-you looks and the grownups would back down. He seemed to know instinctively how to handle parents who felt guilty about disciplining children, and he used his reputation for liberation to his own advantage. Being around Ben was like going to a bad porno movie and not leaving for fear the rest of the audience would think you were a prude.

Nemo and Ellie sometimes came to our house along with Ben, but they never spent any positive time with him—they would deposit him by the television set and come upstairs, light a joint, and shut the door. We never saw them actually discipline Ben, and when crises occurred, they stood on the sidelines with a critical eye for uptightness. If you yelled at Ben they would shake their heads and say, "How can you be so uptight, man? There must be a better way to work it out."

24

Ben stopped coming to the free school after two months. We found out why one day when Nemo and Ellie were driving around in the Mercedes and stopped to roll down their window and announce that Ben was learning at home. "I read to him in bed," Ellie said, which was hard to imagine her doing, "and it's amazing how much he is picking up." Nemo said, "Learning at home is a much better trip. More individual."

It sounded good, except the source made it impossible to take seriously. In the first place, Ben was learning nothing at the school; he functioned particularly poorly in the self-motivating atmosphere. In the second place, the reason Ben had been sent to the school was that he had not acquired reading skills in all those other years at home. It was hard to accept this sudden burst of educational concern on the part of Nemo and Ellie, this sudden support of individualized instruction. Especially since this change in school theory came suspiciously soon after the free school moved location. It was too far for Ben to ride his bike to the new school. There was no bus service, and Nemo and Ellie did not have a reputation for getting up in the morning.

Nemo and Ellie visited us again after some people from a consciousness-raising group called Arica came to Miami. Nemo, who always talked about his psyche as if it were the weather report ("It isn't together yet, man," "It's scattered energy," "It's coming together," or "It's building up")—especially if you wanted him to do something and he would have to wait until the cumulonimbus hit him—said he and Ellie had decided to take a two months' Arica guru-training course in New York to clear their heads up. The course claimed to take the mind through higher stages as surely as a boat rises through the locks of the Panama Canal; the only trouble was that it cost six hundred dollars per person, which Nemo and Ellie didn't readily have. The problem was how to raise this money, and Nemo said Ellie would have to go back to work. "What about Ben?" "Oh," Nemo said, "he is happy in St. Croix. It's a groovy place and he has friends there." "St. Croix? Did he want to go?" "Well," Nemo said, "not at first, but he's into it now." So Ben had been sent to the island to live with an acquaintance of Ellie's while his

25

mother went back to work as a hooker to make money to invest in her consciousness. So she could be a better person. Unfortunately, she had to violate her pact about never leaving his side, but she was sure the end result would be better for him and for her.

"Ben can handle it," Nemo said. "He's a free kid, a far-out kid." In the end, it was clear why Nemo wanted to see Ben that way: he wanted Ben to be liberated enough and strong enough so that he didn't need parents. If his consciousness were high enough, if he would be far-out enough, then Nemo and Ellie could do what they pleased without having to worry about their effect on Ben. Their emphasis on Ben's freedom was just another way of saying, "If he can do anything, then we can do anything." A difficult enough program for a grownup, but especially difficult for a ten-year-old boy who already spent too much of his time searching for his father.

If Ben was the sex child, then Nina was the drug child. Her house was a tip-off among the pruned hibiscus and the sprinkler systems on one of the most exclusive streets in Miami Beach. The grass was never cut and there were old cars in front like you see in movies about Appalachia and the entire front of the house was covered with a hand-painted mural of flower children tripping.

Nina's mother said she took acid every day. It was hard to tell anymore. It got to the point where Bettina, the mother, lost so much weight that she could be a live model for a class in stick figure drawing. We used to take bets on whether she would get skinnier the next time we saw her—how could she and remain alive—but she always did. "The next time we saw her" didn't happen very often, since Bettina left her house only about once every six months. Seeing her in the grocery store was a kind of rare event, like sighting one of the last bald eagles out of captivity. The last time she visited our house was Christmas, when she walked in and handed us a banana and a copy of the 1904 census of London, hugged each of us, and left. These visits were always unsettling, even though they lasted about five minutes and Bettina rarely talked. She has a habit of mimicking the facial movements of whoever is trying to talk to her, squinching her mouth around and flipping her eyelids and jerking her arms as if she is receiving massive electrical shocks about every fifteen seconds. The things she says, you remember. The only thing she ever said to me was, "Kids, kids, kids. You want to know about kids. You want to have a straight kid, then be a freaky mother." She flipped her eyelids three times and threw her arms around herself as if enveloping her body in an invisible cape. Then she left.

Nina's other adult authority figure was Sy, who has been Bettina's boyfriend for about five years. The real father lives in California, but Nina, who was ten, didn't get to see him much. Sy is an ex-lawyer in his early thirties, and gets the money to live in this expensive neighborhood from his father, an ex-jockey who got rich in the Florida land boom. Sy is a tall man who wears cowboy clothes and has a ponytail and never shaves, giving him the appearance of a prospector. He spends his days making deals of different kinds, using his old lawyer connections to get people out of jail, and being Bettina's link to the sane world. He is not exactly sane by the standards of a government agency, but he can make it to the store. His forays into the outside world have to do with prospecting for various drugs. He starts out in the morning, hoping for some acid or opium or coke, and as the day progresses and those fantasies diminish, he develops a cold and calls his doctor for some Robitussin, and if that doesn't work, he develops a toothache so the dentist will give him some nitrous oxide, or he visits a friend in the hospital to see what they have—anything—in their cabinets, and on bad days by the afternoon he settles for snuff. Sy is very friendly and hospitable—he was always sticking small spoons with powder on them in the area of our nostrils and telling us to breathe in. He came on like the Fuller nostril man.

How has all this affected Nina? Her original relationship to us, to our house, was as a deprived child to a welfare agency. She would come over, looking much too skinny and emaciated for a ten-year-old, as if she were suffering the effects of her mother's habit. The minute she arrived in the house, she would go for the refrigerator, or if we were eating she would sit right down at the table, and sometimes she could be seen leaving with a pile of frozen hamburgers. Margie, the woman with whom we shared the house, was Nina's occasional meal ticket, her movie tickets and Saturday ice-skating ticket and ticket to the circus. Margie's was the place where Nina could go swimming and meet other children and pretend to lead a fairly conventional life.

We did not know, at first, how desperately Nina tried to live a conventional life. You wouldn't have thought it possible, going through her house where the decor could be described as Empty Acid Freak, no furniture downstairs except a sodden couch, the walls bare of any ornament except pencil scribbles. We got to see her room once, and we were amazed—there in the middle of that weird house was the perfect ten-year-old-girl's room from the Sears showcase; she had teddy bears and lace curtains and a gingham bedspread, her hairbrushes and mirrors laid out on a vanity, everything clean and put away, and Nina had done it all herself, created this little American refuge. It was the reverse of what most American parents have to fear, that somehow drugs and chaos will seep through the respectable rooms and images that they try to provide for their children; in this case, it was the respectable image seeping through the drugs.

I tried to interview Nina about drugs, thinking that the arsenal she lived in must have affected her in some way. I was playing backgammon with her and said, "What do you think about coke, have you ever tried it?" and she answered, "Yes, I like Coca-Cola." She knew what I was talking about, but Nina liked to put people on. She also was not the slightest bit interested in drugs— her mother said that Nina could take whatever she wanted, but she never wanted to.

It was difficult for Nina to make her life conform to the version portrayed by her room. She had genuine interests (but where did they come from?) in science, photography, and ice skating, but nothing was organized for her; she had to find out schedules and get to places on her own. She never complained about her life at home, and pretended that everything was all right, but at ten she had the kind of responsibility that a day nurse has living with invalids. Not only did she look for food from time to time, but she also took care of her three-year-old brother, Tycho, who was not yet toilet-trained and did not yet know how to talk. He probably had never heard talk. Tycho had been fed a lot of drugs by Bettina but it was never clear whether the drugs affected him, or whether he was naturally adapting to his freaky environment. In any case, it was work for Nina. Once, we found her on our living-room couch in the morning; she was very reluctant to tell us why. Finally, it came out: Tycho had shit in her bed, and nobody had cleaned it up all day, and Nina couldn't bear the thought of it. So she sneaked over in the middle of the night to sleep at our house.

Nina had been living in the acid house for five years and her attendance at school during the first four grades was sporadic. She was allowed to decide for herself whether she wanted to go to school, but to go meant getting up herself and fixing breakfast (if there was anything to fix) and dealing with her three-year-old brother and feeding the dog and getting on the school bus while everybody else was asleep. She had gone to free schools, but Margie enrolled her in a Montessori school to help her catch up in reading and math. Nina would show up at school for a month and then drop out for a month. She knew how to read simple materials and some basic math, but she was far behind other children her age in the basic subjects and very sensitive about it. I tried to teach her some math but she would lose interest at the first difficulty, and pretend she already knew how to do it. The remarkable thing was that she was involved at all in school. Through all the chaos presented by her parents, her impetus to achieve survived just like the dolls and the gingham bedspread.

Nina shared one unmistakable quality with Ben—her hostility toward grownups. She already knew how to make people nervous by using the twitchy eye movements her mother invented. She could put on the appearance of being deferential or polite, partly because she depended on us for so many tickets. But un-

derneath that, she was completely unwilling to follow instructions. She was the one to lead Chauncey and Bernsie into the
pool after being told never to go in without a grownup, and to
teach Chauncey how to run through the house picking up spare
quarters from desks and tables, and use the quarters to buy
candy and bubble gum cards. Nina also had a smartass answer
for everything, which she would put out with the perfunctoriness
of an astronaut and then sit back and watch for a reaction. She
reserved a lot of these answers for questions about life in her
house; in all the talks with Nina, she never mentioned any problems at home.

We liked Nina and attributed her bad behavior to the unre-
solvable tension between her fantasy life and the limitations of
her house. It was even more difficult that Nina's fantasy was a
normal life for most children, a life that she could see happening
all around her. As Sy and Bettina descended further into their
drug stupor, Nina started talking about her party. It was unclear
when she invented the idea, but it was going to be a big party
for all her friends, with a long table and white tablecloth and
streamers and barbecue and plenty of cake and ice cream. She
didn't say where she wanted to hide Sy and Bettina and all the
drugs and the scribbles on the walls, but the party was going to
be held at her house. The more desperate things got at home,
the more elaborate the plans became. Until the day Bettina was
carted off to the hospital with an overdose of something (she
survived) and Nina came over to visit during the trouble, talking
about an even more ambitious gathering for "fifty or sixty" kids
with a merry-go-round and a hired pony and a piñata.

Nina also talked increasingly about moving in with her father,
a man who lived in California and whom she regularly saw only
one week out of the year. Nina always spoke very highly of her
father, about his job in an accounting firm, and about how he
taught her things like how to play backgammon and chess.

Bettina ignored her daughter's frequent requests to go to California. It was obvious that she loved Nina in her own way and
didn't want to lose a daughter. But Nina kept pressing, and

finally Bettina relented. Nina packed up her tidy little room and joined her father.

Ben and Nina's lives revolved—separately—around sexual freedom and drug-taking, the two most publicized aspects of the 1960s revolt. But it was LuAnne who had the most connections to the counterculture. Through LuAnne it became apparent that there could be a direct link between free schools and people who hung around nomadic communes like the Maya House. We met her, coincidentally, in both places. LuAnne was attending the free school (a place that fit her mother's belief that a kid should do only what she wants to do) and living at Maya with her mother, a woman named Sandy.

LuAnne also dispelled, quickly enough, the idea that the counterculture is a kind of unified entity. She and her mother got into a big argument over LuAnne's running off from school to be with the Hare Krishnas. The Hare Krishnas are those shaved chanters you see in most major cities these days, generally considered to be another freaky remnant of the 1960s and, as such, in league with all the other freaky remnants. But apparently this was not the case, because Sandy came storming into the school one day demanding to know why the school had let her daughter skip school to be with the Krishnas. The school said they knew nothing about it, they just assumed that LuAnne, like the other children, was free to come and go as she pleased. Her daughter's visiting the Krishnas seemed to affect Sandy like a country mother who finds out her kid is down at the pool hall, or a psychiatrist who has been informed that his son has quit college to join the Jesus freaks. Sandy accused the school of not taking care of her daughter. She accused the Krishnas of trying to kidnap her daughter. She accused LuAnne of deliberate defiance. Sandy even took LuAnne out of the free school.

LuAnne, at age six, was a very defiant little girl. Like the other two children, she had the ability to exude thorniness when confronted with authority. Susan once met LuAnne at the stove in the free school kitchen. LuAnne said she wanted to help cook. Susan told her to add a little salt; LuAnne poured in a whole shaker. Susan warned her to keep away from the flame, LuAnne moved her chair nearer. Susan said "stir carefully" and LuAnne jerked the ladle around until spaghetti slopped over the sides of the pot. The Krishna incident was just a more extreme example of LuAnne's overall attitude—she even looked scary. She always wore long smocks and no shoes, her hair was uncombed, giving her the appearance of an old inmate at an understaffed insane asylum. At school, she played alone. At the Maya House, she stood out among the clump of swaying, plantlike people. She was the only person in the whole blissful place who scowled. When we met her at the Maya House, she kept repeating, "I'm a devotee" (pronouncing it "divoatee") and giving off various Krishna chants. Even though her mother had removed her from the free school to avoid Krishnas, by some bothersome coincidence the Krishnas had moved their compound right across the street from the Maya House. "Why," Sandy said, "does she do it?"

Sandy and LuAnne occupied a small guest house in back of the Maya garden, where the floor was covered with sleeping bags and still-lit candles and the walls were plastered with Meher Baba posters. There were always dozens of people in there, passing from one place to another—no chance for privacy. Nobody stayed at Maya for too long—Sandy and LuAnne had been there for about two months, since arriving in Florida from a similar encampment in California. Sandy didn't look like she belonged among the gauze robes and stoned stares. She dressed up in flamenco skirts and wore hard red shoes, and painted her face for parties. When asked why she was hanging out at Maya, she said it was rent-free, so she only had to work part-time to support herself. But mostly, she said, it was good for LuAnne, her only child and constant traveling partner. She explained the advantages of Maya the same way Nemo had explained Ben's life— it was a free place, an unencumbered place, a place with no hassles. "Everything is shared here," Sandy said, "even people. There are no private possessions, or possessiveness. I don't want LuAnne to grow up with those hang-ups."

On a physical level, it was obvious what Sandy meant. There were no toys, no books, nothing in either of the houses that could remotely provide a material attachment for a child. LuAnne owned nothing but two dresses and a blanket, she shared a room with as many as twenty people, and she had no room, closet, or box where she could hoard private treasures. On an emotional level, we could sense that Maya House people did not recognize nuclear families or couples; they hugged us and rubbed perfume on our faces in a vaguely threatening way, in what felt like an emotional rape. Sandy said they were working toward a pure form of love, a love that did not rely on marriage certificates or protected families, that if energy is interchangeable in the universe, then "we are all part of the same thing." LuAnne, she said, would have an easier time loving everybody because "she is starting earlier, and growing up freer than we did."

Freedom, Sandy said, was very important to LuAnne. Like most parents looking for safety factors in new houses and signs of accreditation in new schools, Sandy looked for places that would provide LuAnne with leeway. "The best place was a free school in California," Sandy said, "where the only rules were no chemical foods and no balling in the hallways. LuAnne loved it there. It's almost as good at the Maya House, except we get a lot of folks through here and some of them are uptight about what LuAnne does." LuAnne was allowed to eat when she wanted, sleep in strangers' trucks, even take short trips with people who were passing through. It seemed that the only thing Sandy didn't want LuAnne to do was to pretend she was a Krishna. And for some reason mysterious to Sandy, that is exactly what LuAnne did.

LuAnne also had a curious relationship to possessions, or to the lack of them. We visited Maya during our original contact with the nomads, and watched LuAnne at play with Hector and Tree.

Chauncey and Bernsie and Hector and Tree played very well together in the back room at Maya. The only minor disturbances, in fact, came from Chauncey and Bernsie, who grabbed back some of their toys and protested, "It's mine," but were then convinced by the others to share. Hector and Tree seemed peaceful and tranquil and very good at sharing other kids' possessions. They did not have any of their own.

When LuAnne burst into the room, the happy calm was broken. Tree had been wearing a hair dryer while she played, and LuAnne reached over and ripped it off her head. Since, as Sandy had told us, "everything belongs to everybody, even people," there was no clear definition of territory in the matter of the dryer, but LuAnne said she thought it was hers since she had lived at Maya longer. Tree let LuAnne have her way, without even a word of protest, but Sandy, who had been taking a shower in an adjacent bathroom, came in to find out what was happening. When she found out, she asked LuAnne, "Wouldn't you like to give Tree back the dryer until she's finished?" as if to pretend that LuAnne had a choice, but before LuAnne even had a chance to refuse the offer, Sandy's judiciousness turned to anger. She grabbed the dryer out of her daughter's hand and gave it back to Tree. Sandy stared at LuAnne as if to say, "You selfish little bitch," and LuAnne kicked at the toys on the floor and started screaming, not like a regular child's scream, but more like a howler monkey. Sandy grabbed LuAnne by the arm and threw her out of the house, yelling, "I can't stand any more of your bullshit." LuAnne yelled back "Hare Krishna," as if it were an epithet, and headed off in the direction of the street.

LuAnne ran by the hugging people outside and through the trees. She looked behind her as if to make sure somebody was watching, stopped at the side of the road, put her hands out, and walked across like a somnambulist. When I caught up to her, I realized that her eyes were closed. "You could have been hit by a car." She scowled at me like an umpire defending a call. "Lord Krishna protects me from cars," she said, and disappeared into the compound.

Later she was back, running around the garden, obviously not wanting to talk to anybody. The Krishnas didn't want to deal with her either. She disrupted their totally regimented world, the opposite of the Maya House, where every moment was regulated in prayer or cooking or chanting. One of the Krishnas told us, "When things are tough at Maya House, LuAnne comes here chanting 'Krishna.' When things get tough here, she goes home, chanting 'Mommy.' "

One incident with LuAnne's temper could have been ignored (we had been around Bernsie long enough to be accustomed to tantrums). But in three or four days at Maya House, they were frequent and violent. The people in one of the Volkswagen busses threw LuAnne out for cutting up their blankets with scissors when they refused to let her have one. There was an encounter outside the Krishna compound, a repetition of the hair dryer scene, when LuAnne attempted to take a toy box from one of the Krishna children named Marcy. When Susan gave the box back to Marcy, LuAnne bared her teeth like a baboon under attack. She grabbed a stick at Susan's feet. Not to hit her, but to prove that she could take something. "This is mine," she said. "You can't have it."

LuAnne was the upsetting force at Maya House, the jolt in the eternal stupor. Perhaps because of the blissful background, where people never said anything more violent than "I love you" to each other, LuAnne's torments were exaggerated. But a kind of fear of her was universal there. One of the girls in the garden said LuAnne was an evil spirit, a sorceress, and Hector's mother observed that people should stay away from her. LuAnne "was on her own trip," which is a hippie's diplomatic way of saying somebody is screwed up.

Among the huggers and strangers, there was little positive interest in LuAnne or curiosity about the source of her torments. They stayed away from her or they yelled at her. And LuAnne spent her days scratching desperately in a world of nonpossessiveness for one possession that she could hold onto. Whatever she staked out could not be hers.

Sandy was aware of LuAnne's problems, but she said it was because LuAnne was such a free child—people weren't used to handling that. Susan said, "But you get pissed off at her a lot. If she is a free child, then how can you get mad at what she does?" Sandy didn't answer, she just said it was difficult to be at Maya with LuAnne when everybody was against her, and that it was "impossible for a single woman to raise a healthy child." "But you have all these people who could help you." "Yeah. But they are on their own trip."

In this carnival of strangers and passers-through, we never saw Sandy and LuAnne together except when Sandy was yelling.

The lives of the free children were in a shambles. From the promise of a life of no attachments, here were three uniformly depressing situations. Nina, at least, could go off to live with her father, but the other two—when last seen—were floundering desperately for some parental attention. LuAnne had to go all the way to the Krishnas to get her mother to react; Ben had not yet even found a method. Whatever they did, it was not with the joy of a people released from cultural bondage.

It is possible that Ben and LuAnne and Nina merely had uncaring parents. Parents have managed to ignore children, in one way or another, long before there was a counterculture. But the rhetoric of the 1960s justified the inattention of these particular parents so completely that it was impossible to ignore. It was the rhetoric of "not laying a trip" that allowed Nemo and Sandy to transform the ugliness of their indifference into something that they saw as positive. They were giving their children the basic gift of autonomy and independence. Straight parents, by comparison, were destroying their children through their repressive expectations.

So much for how Sandy and Nemo saw things. The idea of freedom, as applied to their children, seemed like an unworkable remnant of the 1960s. As unworkable as another popular 1960s idea—that you could have open marriages without jealousy. There is no such thing as a free child, or a child unencumbered by his parents' limitations. The three examples of free children, in fact, were as bound by their parents' limitations as any children we knew.

Yet it wasn't as if Nemo and Sandy and Ellie were out in left field with their ridiculous beliefs—they were only the most complete practitioners of a child-rearing ethic that attracted the other free school parents and a lot of friends who fashion themselves to be modern, progressive thinkers. The fantasy that a child can be liberated by his own parents, that a child can be unstuck from his own parents, that a child can be unstuck from his own culture, was popular among the hip fringes of a big city. Among parents who toyed with the concept of unstructured schools, and who were unsure about what their children should learn. Among parents who were ambivalent about sexual morality and paralyzed on questions of discipline. There was a general confusion among these parents who knew what was wrong about the way they had been raised, but did not know for certain what to put in its place. To be fair, we didn't know how to deal with Nina and Ben and LuAnne any better than their real parents did. These three children could all intimidate grownups into letting them get away with things. You sensed discomfort around them, you might not like them to throw things or act hostile or make smartass remarks, but you let them get away with it for fear of being called a fascist. A lot of parents around us believed that any direct attempt to stifle a child's behavior was evidence of incipient fascism.

So much has been written about freeing children, freeing them from sex roles and social restraints and how revolutionary that all is, that we believed Ben and LuAnne and Nina to be examples of radical children. Children's rights, interestingly enough, was scheduled to be one of the chapters in this book. It never occurred to us then that rural commune people, at the other end of the counterculture, would put down Ben and LuAnne as fucked-up city kids. Or that children's rights would be viewed by our later contacts as a citified myth, an invitation to self-centered ego-tripping on the part of children. We heard about one commune in Vermont where the children had been allowed the total freedom to live alone in their own barn and make all their own decisions and spurn the influence of grownups. The children burned down that particular commune. Somewhere down the counterculture trail from the Miami people, the word "freedom" —as defined in the lives of Ben, LuAnne, and Nina—dropped out of the language.

❧2❧

The Political Radicals

The free people viewed the change to a new culture much like
the man in the Kawasaki ad. It involved a personal decision—
anybody could do it. You just walk out of the office (and all it
implies), loosen your tie, jump on a motorcycle, outrun the uptight commuters, bypass your suburban home, shed your clothes
and your inhibitions, and end up with Abbie, naked in the
stream. Once you let go of your job and your watch and your
possessions and all that bullshit, then everything else would be
easy. Raising children, getting through the day, would all take
care of itself. Life at the Maya House (which was not really a
commune but a crash pad), and at Nemo's house, exuded this
sense of radical ease. Nobody admitted to working on anything,
it was unfashionable to deal with problems, and the problems
stacked up on Ben like dealer's chips.

This idea of shedding America, on a personal level, was not
accepted by all the people in what we call "the movement." Political radicals took a diametrically opposed stance—that the new

revolutionary world could come only after sacrifice and social struggle and ideological purification. The political movement was so demanding, in fact, that few children were born into it—they were seen as counterrevolutionary and a waste of time. You didn't see Fidel Castro dragging a baby carriage around the Sierra Maestra and you didn't see many Weatherpeople doing it, either.

It seemed that Dylan McKay would be one of the most unusual children in America. He was like an only child to the revolution. He was born into the Red Family, fifteen or so college-educated Americans who declared themselves, in 1967, to be a Maoist collective. It was a bizarre declaration—hardly anybody, in 1967, knew what a Maoist collective was. The baby-sitter would arrive, Dylan's mother said, and all fifteen parents would troop past her, carrying gas masks and riot gear and boxes of bandages on their way to People's Park.

Dylan's mother is Charlotte McKay, a woman who was invited to Hanoi while our bombs were still falling. His father is Robert Scheer, a leftist theoretician who was thought to be even more radical than *Ramparts,* the magazine that published the first works of the Black Panthers. In the middle 1960s, Scheer was one of the first writers to describe America as a brutal police state. It was a scary account of how police took him and held him face down on the pavement with guns aimed at his head and made him stay that way all night—groveling and walking on all fours and making the animal noises the policemen forced him to make. He feared for his life. Scheer and his friends were pioneers in a total disbelief in America—they saw the evil and corruption and brutality reaching right up to the privileged white level and decided to identify with the Chinese.

Dylan was born in 1967, when the Red Family was established in a large communal house in Berkeley. The Red Family wasn't known for violent activism (in the SLA mold) but for its collective intelligence—Scheer and then, later, another movement leader (who was Charlotte McKay's boyfriend after she and Scheer split up) were principal spokesmen for draft resisters and campus protesters all over the country. Dylan's consciousness was developed in the brain center of the revolution.

Charlotte McKay gave an account of what Dylan's life was like during those first four or five years. She said he was nurtured on turbulence, constant activity and lots of people around the Red Family, sleeping on the floor, getting arrested and bailed out, planning demonstrations. Even from his crib days, Dylan was more than a bystander to the commotion because all members of the Family were in one way or another involved in his development. "From the beginning, raising Dylan became a political act in itself," his mother said. "There were even debates about the first words he could speak. Should he learn to say 'pig,' or should he learn to say 'policeman'? Some thought he should begin with a pure idea of who the enemy was. Others, including his father, thought he should at least be able to *say* 'policeman'—just in case he ever needed one."

Then came Blue Fairyland, the revolutionary nursery school. Nothing illustrates the care, the conscious planning, that went into Dylan's early life more than the Fairyland. He was three years old, and the Family worried that he had no playmates except grownups. It was hard to find companions for the only child of a feared underground cell. The Family worried that if he were sent to a regular nursery school, where most children go to meet other children, he would be ideologically contaminated, subjected to sexist racist colonialist thinking. So the Red Family took time out from the ramparts to invent an entire school for Dylan's benefit. It would teach the new consciousness. Robert Scheer wrote the primers and workbooks, replacing Jack and Jill with poems from Vietnamese Freedom Fighters and excerpts from *Quotations from Chairman Mao Tse-tung*. A few other families were daring enough to send their children to this anti-American experiment.

In its two years of life, Fairyland became more than a school; it was the center of an entirely new concept of childhood that developed around Dylan. The creeping politicization of everything had caught up to children. There were student niggers, women niggers, and now natal niggers. Somebody had the idea that *white oppressor* could be applied to parenthood as well as international politics. "A funny thing happened," Charlotte McKay said, "I guess because none of the Red Family had much experience with children. The only way they could relate to Dylan was as a member of a minority group, as if childhood were a new division of the Third World." It was understandable; the Red Family had a sense of rebelliousness to uphold, and so much of the fight of the 1960s was described in terms of parents against their children that there had to be a certain discomfort felt by the young rebels now raising a child. The Red Family had to be the Establishment as far as Dylan was concerned, and it made the Family nervous. Discipline became a matter for political debate. Was it oppressive to tell Dylan to clean the table? Were you a colonialist if you ordered him to stop throwing the cereal? There was no agreement.

Fairyland was a way to get around this problem. The plan was to convert the school into a separate nation for children, where the four- and five-year-olds might achieve independence much like an emerging African state. The children would learn to cook, they would sleep in the school at night, extending their life at Fairyland until they no longer had much need to go home. Once the children had conquered their underdevelopment, then the Home Office could let go. Dylan was a candidate for early liberation, but the rest of the Fairyland parents would not accept the plan. "Most of them were divorced people," Charlotte said, "and they couldn't accept the idea of competing with a school for their already divided attentions." Fairyland folded in 1972.

Sitting at Charlotte McKay's dining-room table, one takes in this family history with growing skepticism. It starts with her toes. I couldn't take my eyes off those ten manicured tip-offs, glistening red at the edge of India leather sandals. Were they double agents? Were they imposters? They had obviously taken a counterrevolutionary amount of time to fix up; so had the rest of her. She was tall and beautiful in a resort hotel sort of way, and yet she had just come from a prisoners' rights meeting. The first thing she said was, "Did you hear Abbie got busted?" and it seemed that she must be trapped in somebody else's body.

Then there was the house. It was a large walnut-paneled place with beveled mirrors and fireplaces, in a section of town occupied by tenured professors and people who get large government study grants. The Red Family had disbanded; Charlotte was living with two other women working for the movement. (They still called it that.) There was almost no furniture left in the place, since Charlotte was planning to move across the street and everything was packed away. And yet even in an unsettled condition, the house managed to exude a quiet formality that one expects from dinners with bow-tie liberals from the 1930s. Before we arrived a woman who answered the phone kept telling us we should make an "appointment"—which would have been a dirty word in 1967. Charlotte was obviously working hard enough to require appointments. She was always off to prisoners' meetings or caucuses on women's rights; the movement was not as dead as one might suppose. But by the looks of the house and the inhabitants, the nature of the movement had changed a lot since the first Maoist declarations were taught to Dylan. Most of Charlotte's work was being done in law offices, and it was no longer easy to tell a radical worker from a muscular dystrophy campaigner.

Then there was Dylan. He was now six years old. The boy who we expected to be dressed in black pajamas and doing karate kicks against the banister was comfortably laid out in a brown leather recliner chair, watching "Star Trek." At first when we approached him there was no sign of life, just television cartoon catatonia. But then his mother told him to stand up, and in immediate compliance he managed to squirm out of the chair and face us. He was tall for his age, with fine blond hair, and clean as a child who has just taken a bath. Except Dylan had just spent a full day at school.

While Dylan was standing there, Chauncey (never one to miss an opportunity) grabbed the recliner for himself. But Dylan turned around and said, "It's my chair" with such princely assurance that Chauncey quickly relegated himself to the floor. The floor was cluttered with boxes of toys, Erector sets, and books, not yet packed up for the move across the street. Dylan pointed out that those were his, too, but offered to let Chauncey and Bernsie play with them. There were other instances when Dylan defended his things, not in a selfish way; but it was clear he was not a newcomer to American notions of private ownership.

Dylan, it seemed, was not a newcomer to any American notions. That was the surprise. We expected something different from a Fairyland child, some hint of what the country might have been like if the radicals had succeeded in taking power. Dylan's day went like this: public school in the morning, supervised play in the afternoon, television in the evening, dinner with his mother, then homework. Sometimes, a visit to the ice cream store. A specific bedtime. On summer weekends, trips to their beach house in Bolinas.

There still could be a raging revolutionary hiding out somewhere inside this all-American schedule. But it did not seem so. Compared to the free children, Dylan unfolded as a child with whom any suburban mother could identify. He was well behaved and did what he was told. He liked the privacy of his own room. He liked to read, and he liked to do well in school.

Dylan did not exhibit the resentment of an emerging African state struggling with a colonialist oppressor mother. In fact, he turned out to be something of a momma's boy. The child whose parents were so eager to offer independence hardly ever strayed from mission control. The day we all went to the beach, we stopped off at a restaurant—Charlotte and two adult friends and Chauncey and Bernsie and Dylan and another Berkeley kid named Charlie. The grownups took one table, and the children were told to fend for themselves at another. Chauncey and Bernsie stayed away from the grownup table, probably because they didn't want me to veto their order of apple pie. But Dylan was at his mother's side almost every time I looked up. He would stand there, with a lost look on his face, and ask for help. The soup was too hot, he said, would Charlotte blow on it? Charlotte told him he could very well blow on it himself, and he went away. He was back a few minutes later to complain that he had pricked the roof of his mouth with a toothpick.

The boys went off to spend their allowance (Dylan got fifty

cents) and then we all headed for the beach. Behind us was a sheer bluff, which Chauncey and Charlie, already partners in adventure, decided to scale. Dylan followed them at first, but he kept doubling back to sit on the blanket with his mother and the other grownups. He kept going back and forth, as if he couldn't choose sides between us and them. Finally, when Chauncey and Charlie were already at the top of the bluff, a bruise settled the matter for Dylan. He slipped on a rock about a tenth of the way up, and immediately headed for his mother, thumb in mouth. He stayed close to that blanket, pawing in the nearby seaweed with Bernsie, for the rest of the afternoon.

Dylan's mother confirmed our observations about his shyness and his dependence on her. That's why Dylan was now in the public school, in the first grade, with regular kids and the regular program that the Red Family had worked so hard to spare him from. "His problem isn't what goes into his head," Charlotte said. "He has that all taken care of. It's in getting along with other kids, especially on the playground. He isn't used to a lot of other kids, and he doesn't like to roughhouse that much."

So for the present, Charlotte McKay had abandoned radical purity for the sake of Dylan's personal growth. It was a major change in her thinking; back in the Red Family they saw radical training and personal growth as one and the same thing. She said that watching Dylan was a constant lesson for her, that she could observe him and then try to come to terms with what was really happening during those years of outrage and clenched fists and intractable revolutionary stances.

The unlikely traits exhibited in Dylan, Charlotte McKay said, came directly from his parents. He had been taught tough, revolutionary rhetoric, but that didn't keep him from picking up his father's bookish inclinations, his father's dislike of physical contact. He had been taught self-confidence from fifteen different people who were involved in taking care of him, but that didn't stop one parent (his mother) from imprisoning him on an emotional level. "I realize, in looking back on it," Charlotte said, "that I probably kept Dylan away from other people. I worried about the different influences, that he might get confused, and I

44

held him too much away from the others." Despite all the training in the evils of the American system, Dylan liked to do well in school, to please his teachers. "The men around him were all on ego trips," Charlotte said, "one eye always on the New York *Times*. They had a superstar mentality."

It is not unusual for a child to inherit his parents' character traits. But it was surprising to see such traditional characteristics survive in the Red Family. By the looks and the feel of him, Dylan could easily have come from Darien or Grosse Pointe. His life and his attitudes were remarkably untouched, as if the revolution swept through his family but passed by its most personal and human realities. Dylan did have a protective, middle-class mother and an achieving, educated father and, on an emotional level, their hopes for him were not that different from the hopes of the parents from Darien. It's as if their deeper instincts and fears were transmitted, intact, through all the hoopla about new consciousness and radicalized society, and in effect sneaked through the rhetorical lines. Now that the time of radical posturing was over, Charlotte McKay could consider her son a product of the Red Family and in a sense its only lasting creation. She could consider his needs as a normal American child who in fact did grow up in Darien or Grosse Pointe, a child who liked solitude and public schools and possessions and an ordered existence. She worried, like a suburban divorcée, that Dylan would not trust her future boyfriends since he had been "ripped off" by the men who had come and gone in her life. So in spite of its appearance as a Maoist collective family, the Red Family had really been—for Dylan—a nuclear family, with attendant traditional father-mother-lover problems. To consider the radical movement through Dylan was to consider the ultimate conservatism of parents who had believed that they could change the world without having to change themselves.

Dylan, of course, was essentially an incomplete story. It was obvious what his life was like now, but his early training grounds —the Red Family and the Blue Fairyland—had been disbanded. Were other radical children like Dylan? There weren't enough of them around that it would be so easy to find out. But we did meet a Weathercouple in Berkeley with an eighteen-month-old son. The parents were George and Dorothy, who had met in an underground collective in Pittsburgh in 1969. Both of them had just gotten out of college, and in less turbulent times they might have met in graduate school. As it was, they met inside the Weathermen, popularly known as the bomb-throwing arm of the movement. At one time or another, George and Dorothy were both jailed for political crimes. Dorothy's former boyfriend was killed when a bomb accidentally exploded in a New York Weatherman collective. George was indicted in a celebrated Weatherman case in Wisconsin.

George and Dorothy waited until 1971 to have their baby, and by that time they were aboveground again. George was awaiting trial in the Wisconsin case (later dropped by the government). A lot of their Weatherfriends were scattered like cirrus on the horizon, some in jail, some double-crossed, some in regular jobs, some out of the country, some still underground. George and Dorothy lived in a two-bedroom bungalow in Berkeley with Ernesto, their eighteen-month-old child. George was working for a people's radio station and wasn't home that much, and Dorothy was deeply involved in radical parenthood. Ernesto attended a nursery school three days a week, alternately supervised by different members of Dorothy's consciousness-raising group. One of Dorothy's main acts of new consciousness was making sure that George took part in the routines of baby care. He did the 6 A.M. bottle and several diaper changes a week, and took Ernesto to the park on a schedule assigned to him by Dorothy. While we stayed with them, Dorothy even added a few more chores for George, and although he seemed to resent it in some distant way, he didn't argue; it didn't appear that he was that involved. Dorothy seemed to be constantly searching for ways that George might be taking advantage of her as the male chauvinist parent. As her consciousness was raised, the list of George's chores grew. When she was fully liberated, he would probably be doing everything.

You could tell how much space Ernesto occupied in his parents' lives just by taking a look at the house. The living room was lined with several wooden boxes filled with toys. There were two shelves of children's books to be read on demand, and Ernesto had an entire bedroom to himself with a playpen and a crib. All in all, he took up half the floor space. The walls were partially covered with Vietnam posters, reminders of the struggle, but they were gradually being outnumbered by big elephants and Dr. Seuss drawings and advertisements for "Sesame Street." The Weatherman slogan was on the kitchen blackboard—"You don't have to be a Weatherman to know which way the wind is blowing"—but it was hidden behind the day-care schedule and a diagram of the backyard garden and a list of doctors' appointments. The feeling you got from the house was that Ernesto had succeeded in pushing the movement out of the way.

We spent the day with George and Dorothy and little Ernesto. We were going to go to the beach, but it rained, so we ended up in Sausalito at a hokey little shopping center camouflaged as a fishing village. Ernesto was strapped in his kiddie seat and dressed in his institutional cotton creepers; he talked around a pacifier stuck into his mouth, like a politician with an old cigar. They called the pacifier his yummie, and when he didn't have it in his mouth, George and Dorothy spelled it out, y-u-m-m-i-e, so that Ernesto wouldn't know they were talking about it, and want it.

We all got out of the car and went into a high-priced restaurant overlooking the bay, a place with art nouveau menus and a lot of young, middle-class couples dressed up as hippies. Ernesto sat on a bentwood high chair and chewed on the salt shaker. George and Dorothy did nothing to stop him. Then Ernesto threw the shaker on the floor. They picked it up and gave it back to him. "Now Ernesto," George said, reasoning with the kid, "you can have it, but it really isn't a toy." Next Ernesto pitched it onto the table, with the wry smile of a hockey player driving the puck down a goalie's throat. Salt scattered. "I don't know whether to let him destroy the whole table, or to take it away from him," Dorothy said, in what turned out to be the classic radicals' dilemma. Susan, a little bemused by this time, suggested repression: "You really don't want him to destroy the table, do

47

you?" They decided to take the shaker away from Ernesto. He cried. They gave him a hard roll to replace it, and he threw that on the floor. "Ernesto, you mustn't do that. Do you want another roll? But only if you eat it." He did want one, of course, and he tossed that onto the floor the minute he got his hands on it. Finally, he started to squirm out of his chair and scream. People were watching. George gulped down his coffee and took the little restaurant anarchist outside, while we finally got a minute to eat. Susan asked Dorothy, "Don't you mind that George has to miss his meal like this?" and Dorothy said, "Don't be silly. Weekends are the only time he can spend an adequate amount of time with his son."

Any child can misbehave in a restaurant from time to time, but Ernesto didn't just stop there. He carried the fight everywhere, into the home, throwing blocks at the television set, whining the minute George left to go to the grocery store—incessantly demanding and rarely satisfied. He was only eighteen months old and already he had developed an incredible sense of displeasure with the world. Dorothy would pick him up and talk with him like one good Weatherman to another: "Ernesto, I don't want to be uptight but there is just so much you can destroy; kid, be reasonable." He would give her a John Mitchell chin and go right back to throwing blocks at the TV. Ernesto didn't know what a guerrilla war was, but he already knew how to start one to get his mother's attention.

Was this the beginning of a radical's training, an eighteen-month-old baby with a heightened sense of outrage and a good throwing arm? It was amusing; here was a little baby not yet out of his creepers, and already he was exactly what conservatives had accused the Weathermen of being—a selfish, overprivileged child who threw things to get attention. But Dorothy said she wasn't deliberately teaching Ernesto to be an anarchist, she wasn't deliberately teaching him anything. She didn't know exactly where her beliefs on discipline came from. We couldn't tell either, but we got the impression that Dorothy was instinctually afraid to stand in the way of a child. That impression was finally clarified when Bernsie began to scream about something, and I put her outside the door and told her to come back when she quieted down. Dorothy got very upset, and said it was cruel punishment, how could I do that to Bernsie, and that Bernsie would never forgive me. She was so vehement about it that I began to doubt what I had done. Bernsie, of course, appeared a few minutes later, smiling broadly, and asked me to play with her. It was her way of saying that things were all right. Dorothy still couldn't accept what had happened, and said, "It blows my mind. I would never treat Ernesto like that. I am afraid he would hate me forever."

"Hate me forever" had a familiar ring to it. Susan said she used to worry that Chauncey and Bernsie would hate her every time she said no to them. That was before we went through a certain amount of commune therapy. Dorothy said that her mother had never wanted to say no to *Dorothy*. Which brought up the question of continuity. We wondered what kind of family Dorothy had come from. It was not hard to guess; both Susan and Dorothy were confederates in New York raucousness, in a shrill, impelling self that is classical Jewish princess. Like most of the Weathermen, Dorothy had a well-off family that sent her to college and were interested in her achievement. Besides that, she said she had gotten pretty much her own way with things when she was a child, which was just how it was turning out, so far, with Ernesto. It supported the theory that the cradle of American radicalism is rocked by the fearful, overgiving, permissive mothers of the land.

Dorothy was an avid reader of Dr. Spock. Even though she thought he was a sellout politically, she compared Ernesto's development to the "normal" child described in Spock's chapters, as if cultural and political developments could be kept wholly separate. They were as separate in Dorothy's mind as they had been in Charlotte McKay's. In terms of gut worries, Dorothy had all the common anxieties of motherhood—about Ernesto's health, about whether he was smart, whether he was learning to walk and talk on schedule, whether he was going to the bathroom properly—every inch of his brain and body was already staked out as an area of potential concern.

These were the common, traditional motherhood worries that had been untouched by the Weathermen experience just as so many of Charlotte McKay's traditional attitudes had survived the Red Family. Dorothy's treatment of Ernesto did not come from conscious deliberation on her part. She admitted that. It came from some unreachable emotional source, gut feelings that had not been altered by all those months of living in a collective and plotting to overthrow the system, feelings that revived on the emergence of a child. If you have ever watched a mother in the park when her child disappeared around the corner, that was the look in Dorothy's eyes when she talked about Ernesto and his life.

I had a vision sitting there listening to Dorothy talk (which was hard to do because of Ernesto banging his books on the floor) about a *Ms.* magazine reporter visiting this house, seeing the day-care schedule and how Dorothy managed to get afternoons off from her child, hearing about the Weatherman experience, watching George change the diapers and make the formula, listening to Dorothy describing her upleveled consciousness and opposition to sex roles, and concluding that here, indeed, was a liberated family. But something was wrong with that view, wrong beyond the usual facile put-downs of women's liberation. It had to do with Dorothy's agonies. She was so involved in Ernesto, in pleasing him, in worrying about his physical safety, in buying him things, in fretting about his hating her, that the external liberation seemed irrelevant. Dorothy was not free from a constant preoccupation with her own child. That she had in common with Charlotte McKay of the Red Family. And with Susan and most other mothers in America.

Dorothy was bound to Ernesto in the same cycle of fear and protection that Susan knew so well from her own motherhood. George shared the housework, but when it came down to the emotional work of cringing for Ernesto, Dorothy was alone. Not because it was in the sexist marriage contract that the mother must do all the cringing, but because that is the only way Dorothy knew how to be. She was just another mother whose identity was caught up in her child, who could not consider herself and Ernesto as separate beings. She was able to consider being liberated in the areas of schedules and routines, but it had not touched her reflexes or the guilty buttons that Ernesto already knew how to push. Guilt is what caused Ernesto to get away with so much, and Dorothy did not want to be accused of holding back.

Dr. Spock says that having a child invariably takes you back to your own childhood, which is how a culture is perpetuated, and your reactions as a parent can be involuntary. Neither Dorothy nor Charlotte McKay, during the political phase of the Red Family, had begun to recognize or deal with her involuntary motherhood. Ché and Mao and Frantz Fanon hadn't prepared them to understand that.

We could see, in Ernesto and Dylan, that there is a big difference between being a revolutionary who is a parent and raising a child in a revolutionary manner. To a child, a parent can be nothing but a conservative; the world he is brought into is the only world there is. A child is also the true test of a revolutionary because a child is the creation of his parents. A frustrated revolutionary can always claim that reactionary forces ruined his idealistic plans for making things better. But he cannot claim that for his children. It seemed to us that Dylan and Ernesto blew the cover of the revolution, just like Chauncey and Bernsie often did with us, uncovering our unconscious attitudes and reflexes that we didn't even know we had, revealing our characters in surprising and unsettling ways. The radical movement, in a sense, had denied this kind of personal awareness; the political stance had nothing to do with the relationships between mother and child or friend and friend, the day-to-day things people do to each other. Charlotte McKay had matured enough to recognize that. We learned a lot from her.

There may have been other political families with children, but we decided to leave them behind. After visiting the free parents and the radical parents, separate families no longer interested us. Both groups claimed to have raised their consciousness;

51

but in the case of the free people, that resulted in indifference toward children, and in the case of the radical people, it resulted in no apparent effect at all. All these families had one thing in common—they had not, on the deepest level, learned to share their children. And there seemed to be no course for them between the extremes of frightening disinterest and traditional obsessions. From what we had seen of nuclear families (however apparently radical), they did not provide the mutual criticism, group revelation, and communal support necessary to really alter the way parents deal with their children. We wanted to find parents who had risked much more than either of these two groups, who had altered not only what they thought, but how they loved, worked, lived, and achieved. Parents who had decided not to hold onto their children so selfishly, or abandon them so completely. If there can be a new child only to the degree that there is a new parent, then we wanted to meet people who were raising their *unconscious,* who were fighting the invisible mother and the deeper American instincts that had survived the Red Family and its revolution.

❦ 3 ❧

Urban Communes

The Characters:

Steve, a psychologist and the guru with an Accutron watch
Amy, the communal Jewish mother
Karen, their dumpy nine-year-old daughter

Mary, the divorcée with all the boyfriends
Mark, her oldest son (ten), who shows off his yoga
Michael (seven), who pulls the covers off her lovers

Donnie, the registered nurse who was rarely home
Jack (nine), her daughter who wasn't talking

Bill, a psychologist without a wife
Dixie, his demanding three-year-old daughter

Eloise, the sixteen-year-old runaway who bristles at the term

Assorted walk-ons

Bernsie is about to draw on the living-room wall of the Cosmic Circle commune with a green crayon. Susan interrupts her conversation with Mary, one of the women here, rushes across the room yelling, "Berns, don't do that," and gives Berns the usual two-minute lecture on how paper is for drawing and walls are not for drawing. "I don't have any paper," says Berns. Susan is on the way out the front door to get some paper, her journalistic duties forgotten in the call of motherhood, when Eloise stops her. Eloise is the freckly-faced sixteen-year-old who manages to look as fresh as an airline hostess even when she's wearing a Jimi Hendrix tee shirt. "It's OK," says Eloise. "Why waste your paper? Why waste your time? She can draw on the wall. Everybody else does." And Eloise points to a large expanse of wall on the far end of this massive room they call the Cavern, a wall covered with homemade paintings and penciled graffiti like you find in neglected men's rooms. Berns directs herself to that wall, and her "Duck with Cigar in Mouth" becomes part of the permanent collection of the Cosmic Circle.

We could see immediately how this place had changed families. It eliminated the need for about 90 per cent of the protective sorties we have come to call "parenthood." Children roamed this giant room—created by tearing the walls out of three brownstone houses and connecting them—without a worry of breaking, staining, or reducing the resale value of anything. The sensation of being in this room was like being in a truck of refugees who had piled up their most useful possessions in a hurried flight from a homeland. Form gave way to function on every level. Bicycles hung on the wall instead of paintings. Shoes were thrown in a large cardboard box next to the front door. The dining-room table, a rectangular one that sat twenty people, was often covered with sawdust, carpentry tools, and boards glued together with vise grips. The piano over in the corner was missing some keys, and its top was carved like a public picnic table. The floor was cluttered with used auto parts, darts, empty tobacco cans, discarded record jackets. The couches and pillows, strewn around the room in no particular order, were the kind that only a college freshman would buy from a college senior. It

54

was the first living room where one worried more about what the things might do to children than what the children might do to the things. It was the first place (except for the Maya House) where the physical world of the children had been drastically altered from what most children are used to.

The people who occupied this room were urban professionals who had all emerged, three and a half years ago, from regular houses with walls and Danish furniture and hardwood floors to protect. Some of them still drove to work in the mornings, but you could see from the Cavern that there had been a change of mind. A woman named Mary, whom we first met while she was taking a bath in a porcelain tub that stuck out from under the staircase into the kitchen area, told us she had come here to "simplify her life." The house was bought with cash, she said: the new inhabitants, twenty of them then, did all the wall-ripping themselves, and picked up old furniture from garage sales. "We didn't allow ourselves to keep anything we really cared about," she said. "Later, we discovered some people had stashed their good stuff secretly in bonded warehouses."

Five children lived here (six, if you count Eloise, who was sixteen) without the props that we thought basic to an urban child's life—the props that still filled the entire back end of our car. The five children occupied two of the upstairs bedrooms, bedrooms without any doors. They slept on floor mats, and what possessions we could see in those two bedrooms would not have filled a single large cardboard box. Amy, the forty-year-old matriarch of this place, who wore leftover cocktail dresses and gave the guided tours, was quite proud of the fact that the children had stripped down their "baggage" to a few items of clothing and a bicycle for each of them. Plus the Turtle, of course. The Turtle was collectively owned and managed by the children. It was a large ferrocement structure in the backyard, stocked with food, cots, and a working gas stove, where grownups were forbidden to enter.

For some reason, Amy neglected to show us the garage room full of toys. Michael finally did. Michael was a seven-year-old who grabbed onto Chauncey from the moment we arrived, and the two of them were rarely heard from again. It was a case of two children desperate for playmates. Chauncey and Michael mostly played in a dirt pile next to the Turtle, making toys from sticks and rocks and loose string, but once in a while Chauncey would take Michael into our portable suburb for some factory-made caps or balloons. It was during one of those visits to our car that Michael brought up the "toys in the back room." Michael took Chauncey to the white-shingled garage behind the house, opened the door, and revealed Christmas morning. Incredible piles of stuff gathering dust on the floor—Erector sets, Monopoly games, dolls, swim masks, Lionel trains in triplicate. Michael didn't pick anything up or even suggest playing with it; he just seemed to want to prove that it was there.

"Oh, *that* stuff," Amy later said. "I forget it's out there. When we came here, there were a lot of hassles about what belonged to who, about broken things and who broke them. We had a meeting and decided to relegate the toys to the garage, where the grownups wouldn't be bothered. But, you know, the kids hardly ever go in there. Now it's just a toy drop, a forgotten place to throw the birthday presents that the grandmothers send."

Even in the radical families' homes, there was a sense of order, of structure, and of possession—things were owned, things had a place, things had a meaning. At the Circle commune, toys and boxes of books were not part of the landscape; after Michael showed Chauncey the garage, its door was never opened again during our visit. Possessions were relegated to an unimagined secondary status—it was a common cliché that commune children were more apt to share their things; but here, the entire question of things did not appear to be that important. Things were useful, but not worth fighting for, and we didn't see any fights.

The lack of order in the physical surroundings heightened the impression that these children were being raised in a bus station. Everybody hung out in the big room, there was no privacy, no separation of functions, no orderly pattern of events to describe, no obvious connections between the people. It was a definite part of all communes in the day-in, day-out jumble of new people and confusions that now formed the backdrop for these children's lives. From the first morning, caught in the anarchy of fifteen people trying to cook their own breakfasts, we were totally disoriented. Two men in business suits, Steve and Bill, went out the door like suburban husbands—but husbands to whom? Women and children mingling together, but which belonged to which? Amy introduced us around, but nobody drew dotted lines from one to the other with accustomed phrases like "This is my mother," or "That is my son." I had an intense conversation with a man named Boog, a fat man with a tattoo on his arm who gave me his theories on the benefits of beating children. He neglected to tell me that he had only been here for two months and had no children himself, so his views were irrelevant.

It was extraordinary being in a house for two days and still not being able to fix the relations between all the people. We got to know the children, watching them around the house—Eloise the hostess, always smiling, always fixing things; Jack the aloof nine-year-old, who hung out alone in the Turtle a lot of the time; Michael, who merged with Chauncey; Mark the posturer, who put himself in elaborate yoga contortions on the floor to get attention; Karen the officious, who had a psychological description for everybody and threw words around like "obsessive neurotic" and "compensating for insecurities"; Dixie the three-year-old whiner—long before we were exactly sure which grownups they were related to. Karen was the biggest talker, and she had a habit of calling Amy "mother," so it became quickly apparent that she was the daughter of Steve and Amy. But the others we weren't sure about. Dixie spent most of her time in the corner with Eloise, where Eloise had established a species of one-child preschool, so we thought Dixie and Eloise were somehow related. Jack didn't seem to spend time with any grownup, preferring the solitude of the Turtle, where adults weren't allowed, and parrying probing questions with slightly cynical answers ("Are you a vegetarian?" Susan asked. "No, I'm a sagittarian," Jack said). Mark and Michael glued onto whoever happened along; a visitor to this commune might think they were related to *us*. Anyway, it was two days before we figured out that Eloise ar-

57

rived here by herself, as a runaway; that Mark and Michael were sons of Mary, the woman we met in the bathtub; that Jack was the daughter of Donnie, one of the people who worked during the day and was hardly ever home; and that Dixie was the child of Bill the psychologist, who was likewise absent.

That became part of a definition of communality, how long it takes to decide who belongs to whom. In light of what happened here, it was clear why Maya House had not been a real commune. At Maya, Sandy was loath to use possessive words and extolled her daughter's freedom, but it didn't take more than two seconds to figure out that LuAnne was her daughter. At the Cosmic Circle, different grownups were involved with the children, to the point that it was difficult to connect mother with child. Children were also given more room to work things out on their own—which augmented our difficulty. The little girl Dixie fell down and bumped her head, everybody was in the house, they all heard the thump that usually makes the real parent come running, but nobody came. Dixie sat there at the foot of the stairs, crying in the middle of a pile of shoes, for what seemed like five minutes.

Finally it was Eloise who got up off the floor, came over to Dixie, picked her up and patted her head. The crying stopped. "You couldn't be the mother," I said, knowing that she wasn't. "No," she said. "But we have a rule here. When a child has a problem, the nearest person is the parent."

Aside from the fact that the nearest person to Dixie was always Eloise, the system seemed to work out well. The other children spread out their physical needs among other grownups and among themselves to the point that they could hardly be called a bother. For people who despair at the number of glasses of water they pour for children each day, the number of questions they must answer, the number of times they have to say "don't," this group arrangement had a lot of potential.

We marveled at how sensible and easy these collective arrangements were, how nice it was to be relieved of some of the burdens of caring for Chauncey and Bernsie, until one of *their* children entangled us. It happened on the third day, when Jack,

the somber nine-year-old who so far had said about three words
to us, came to Susan and asked to be taken to the clinic for a tetanus shot. She had no timidity about approaching strangers
when a thing needed to be done. She said she stepped on a nail
outside near the Turtle. "Why us?" Susan asked, and Jack, with
straightforward awareness of our assets, said it was because we
had a car.

Jack took care of her puncture wound in clinical fashion, getting bandages out of a cabinet, putting a pot of water on the
stove, then calling for Eloise to help her dress the wound, and we
were left to consider the risks. When somebody else's child asks
you to get her a tetanus shot, a sense of caution overtakes you.
You are reminded of the nuclear family lines that are crossed at
your moral or legal peril. What if she had a bad reaction to the
shot, or didn't need a shot, then could we get into trouble? More
likely, how would her mother accept that two strangers took her
daughter to get an injection without her knowledge? Especially
since Jack's mother, Donnie, was a registered nurse, we thought
it better that Jack wait for the green light from the mother. Susan
told her so.

"I don't want to wait," she said, not with any petulance, but
as a simple statement of fact.

"Can't we just take you to the hospital where your mother is
working?"

"It's across town. Besides, I'm not speaking to my mother
right now."

That made it sound even worse. We were caught in the throes
of a family squabble. Maybe Jack was setting this thing up to
make her mother mad, and we were the unwilling accomplices.
So we stood there, hemming and hawing over the patient, not
knowing whether to trust her. The bottom line was that we didn't
trust nine-year-old children to take medical decisions into their
own hands.

"It's no big deal," Jack said, soaking her foot and sensing our
indecision. "All you have to do is *drive* me to the clinic. They
know us there. We aren't supposed to walk to that neighborhood."

Jack was a very persuasive person and, in her lean fourth-grade frame, had a compelling kind of confidence. But I still don't think we would have done it, if Amy, the commune matriarch, hadn't come over and said it was all right. It changed our whole relationship with Amy—she had treated us as fellow travelers, I think because we looked funky, but now she began to treat us with mild condescension. We were not equipped to deal with a simple tetanus shot or a child's word for it.

It was an opportunity to get Jack away from other people long enough to talk to her, but on the way to the clinic, she reverted to being uncommunicative, a slight presence slumped up against the back door. She answered our questions with the enthusiasm of an applicant at the welfare office. She liked the commune, she didn't like the food, she didn't like her mother, she liked Eloise. These were all openings, conversational invitations that Jack ungraciously refused. She perked up only once, at the sight of a 7-Eleven store, when she got interested enough to ask if we would stop to get some ice cream. She relegated us to a position of aides. "At home we aren't into ice cream that much," she said, gobbling down her Sealtest sandwich.

We expected some reaction to the tetanus shot affair from Jack's mother, Donnie, a lady who wore Earth Shoes and brown baggy clothes and examined her feelings like a Quaker. But we didn't mention it, and she didn't mention it, and after a while, we thought she might be angry and afraid to tell us. Finally we cornered her (she wasn't home too much) and discovered that Jack hadn't even *informed* Donnie about the tetanus shot. It didn't appear to bother the mother, who said something about how it gave her a good feeling to know that Jack had friends to help out. What she didn't say was, "Oh, my god, I wonder what other shots this kid is getting without telling me"; Jack's autonomy on that level didn't concern her.

How can you accept sharing the basic responsibility for your children? It wasn't as simple as shared baby-sitting, which is how we had envisioned the advantages of communes. And it wasn't as simple as at Ben's house, where everybody could share in avoiding the children by repeating, "They're on their own trip, man." Here people dealt directly with other people's children, and to do that, they had to give up some of the preemptive parental rights that Susan and I still believed in. Well, we hadn't known how much we believed in them until the tetanus shot episode. Mary, a vivacious-looking woman who had been one of the founders of this place, said that was one of the hardest things about living here, letting other people deal directly with your children. That and sexual jealousy. "One thing that happened when we first got here," she said, "was people would yell at my kids [Mark and Michael] or take a swat at them, and I got pissed off. It got so that when somebody else would tell Michael to do something, he would turn around and say, 'You can't tell me, you're not my mommy.' We discussed how to get him beyond this notion, and Steve suggested that *I* was the problem. I denied it at first, but later I had to admit it. I liked Michael saying that, it gave me a certain sense of my power over him. I mean, I still had him in some special way. It's hard to give that up."

There were a lot of theories about how these children were different than they had been in the nuclear families into which they had been born. The most repeated was Amy's theory, that the Circle children were "growing themselves up." That meant a lot of things—Jack's being able to stay in the Turtle and cook her own meals there, Eloise's responsibility for the little girl Dixie, all the children's freedom to decide when to go to bed, what to wear, whom to sleep with, and even whether or not to go to school. Jack, Eloise, Mark, Michael, and Karen had all these choices, but the difference between their freedom and what was allowed at Maya House was that misbehavior was no longer a sign of liberation at the Cosmic Circle. "We went through that bullshit in the beginning," Amy said, "letting them run all over us. But we couldn't keep a house together that way." Here there were penalties for fighting, stealing, breaking things, not working. Usually, Amy said, the penalty was isolation. And here the children had a lot of work to do.

They began to work after Bill and Steve and Donnie had left for their outside jobs, and Mary and Amy and Eloise and assorted adult floaters would sit in a corner and talk. The talk mostly centered around psychological interactions, so the feeling you get from the children sweeping and dusting around these people, is of janitors at Esalen. Michael, the seven-year-old, would carry plates in from the big table, would try to impress Chauncey as to how many he could carry at once. Jack would scrape and start the dishwasher, and complain about the number of plates and why didn't they use paper ones. Mark would sweep for a while, always shooting an extra puff of dust in the grown-ups' direction, and then take down a big canful of grass and begin rolling joints. It took awhile to realize that this was a regular job, and was listed on the sign-up sheet for daily chores. At first, it seemed like one of Mark's perpetual bids for extra attention.

Mark was the one we figured would be least involved in the chores of the house, because he was the least serious of all the children. Jack was snippy but very earnest, Eloise was committed to the point that she said, "I want to stay here forever," and Karen was never around the house enough for us to watch her. But Mark was visible, a mischievous ten-year-old, always planning tricks like putting water buckets over doorsills, bothering Boog the carpenter by constantly asking him to ripple his tattoo. When I saw Mark alone one day, outside painting a tool shed, bare-chested with his shark's-tooth necklace clinking against the side of the paint can, I thought it was a good opportunity to hear some complaints about the Cosmic Circle. I approached him and asked, "How do you like all this work around here?" Mark had a smartass answer for a lot of things; I expected he would have a smartass answer about all the work. But he didn't follow that script. "It's good to help out," he said, dipping his brush and looking, for the moment, innocent. "That's how we keep this place going."

Standing on the ladder just below him, I felt completely out of touch, like a man who had just told a dirty joke and gotten no response. I thought you could count on that from the children, the joking about the dishes or painting the house or doing the lawn. It was part of the formula, later to develop into jokes

62

about being married and having to work instead of watching the football game. But something had been short-circuited here. Mark could joke about women and chemical foods and smoking grass ("I don't smoke anymore," he would often say, "I'm on a natural high now") but he took his housework very seriously.

"What happens if you don't get it done?" I asked. "Different things," he said. "Once I didn't cook dinner when I was signed up, I just forgot. Everybody went out and had pizza. I had to stay home."

There was nothing strenuous about the work here, but the way the children went about it, one could sense a new attitude. The difference between helping and working. Helping is when the children's chores become more tedious for the grownups than if the grownups did them themselves. Helping out, in our experience, resulted in soap on the floor, broken Windex bottles, half-made beds, and a lot of nagging questions from Chauncey and Bernsie. Of course, they were younger than these children. But what impressed us here was that Circle children did not help out. They worked. Their jobs were part of the regular "rotation sheet" for the day, not token chores to be later completed by parents.

But too much can be made of this working thing. The Circle children stretched out their jobs with a certain solemn flourish because they had little else to do. They weren't going to school. Well, Karen, Steve and Amy's daughter, was attending the public school, but we hardly ever saw her. The rest stayed home. Amy said it was their own decision, they had freely chosen it. It was the first year they had been allowed to do that.

Steve the psychologist had gone to the local school board and used his credentials to convince them that the commune could provide a tutored education to those who stayed home. That was at the beginning of the year when, as Amy told us, "lots more people were here and we thought we could put together our own school." Now it was March, and most of those other people had drifted away, and the only tutor left was Eloise, who had not finished high school herself but said she didn't care. She had set up a blackboard and piano and shelfful of books in one corner of the room. There was a sign-up sheet for lessons in math and in English, and the last entry was for January 20. Eloise's only real student was three-year-old Dixie, who demanded to be read Dr. Seuss books.

Since the older kids had to decide between staying home or going to public school on a year-to-year basis, they were stuck with their decision at least for this year. Karen had chosen to go to school, but we wondered how free that choice had really been, since her parents were the commune's oldest members and obviously the most academically inclined. The other children had admittedly fallen behind. Mark had missed the entire fifth grade and was floundering with his reading. The only thing we saw him try to read was comic books. Michael, his brother, had missed second. Jack had missed fourth, and she said she was sorry about that. "I don't want to be put back a grade."

The mothers of the children who stayed home, especially Mary, had replaced their former faith in school with a faith in the garden. Mary said it didn't matter that Mark and Michael weren't keeping up, that "they are learning to be self-sufficient so they can learn to survive." They were learning, she said, from the backyard garden, from the chicken and the duck, from doing their chores, and from Boog the carpenter. It was a nice fantasy, but it didn't support what was actually happening. Mark hung out with Boog, but only to admire his tattoo or talk to him about his gypsy exploits. Michael spent time with the chicken, but only to chase it, not to feed it. Jack didn't have anything to do with any of it. Boog knew where it was at, skillwise; he called Mark a "klutz who will never know a nail from his asshole." The children worked on the garden, when required, but it didn't take much to care for six tomato plants and four squash hills and a couple of rows of carrots. It certainly wasn't going to make this family self-sufficient when the world collapsed. The Circle garden was more like a family pet than a source of food.

So in spite of Mary's hopes and in spite of the household chores, the days at the Circle were imbued with listlessness for the children, a state of affairs which resembled that in many other urban communes. The children were all occupied to a certain degree—Jack in carrying on an elaborate snub of her mother, Donnie; Michael in playing with Chauncey; Eloise in being a super housewife to everybody. But the alternative life was not a full life for most of them. Mark especially had never really adjusted from the days of a waiting mother and a car at his disposal and the baseball practices and plays and school activities that once had filled up his days. (He and his mother had been at the Circle for three years.) We became his action for the week, and he depended on us to take him to the store, the park, and movies. He showed us yoga positions, and complained about the "chemical shit food" we had stocked with our camping gear in the back of our car.

Other neighborhood children didn't come over to the Cosmic Circle. Amy said it was because the Circle people were so "far-out," and talked like they were in danger of being thrown out of town any minute. She made us promise we wouldn't identify the city where the commune was located. It's true, the house appeared a little odd, but the people looked and talked like other professionals in their middle thirties, and Steve and Bill and Donnie were close enough to the regular world to hold down good jobs. Amy exaggerated the daring of the living experiment, like people who hoped their phones were tapped. But her sense of paranoia and cynicism was shared by the children, who never ventured down the street and were not visited by neighbors from what even Mark called "the bullshit materialistic, ego-tripping, asshole world."

When asked if he missed school, Mark predictably said, "No, it's bullshit." Everything was pretty much bullshit with him. But I had a feeling he did miss it, an excuse to hang out with other children, and that he and Jack and Michael would be back in school next year.

What were the grownups doing while the children were bumbling around inchoately? They were talking. In fact, the main purpose of the Cosmic Circle seemed to be analyzing every nuance of every relationship. They weren't really into the garden, as Mary said, or into survival, they were into the psyche. Maybe it was because the place was kept alive, economically, by

Steve and Bill, the two urban psychologists. Bill said what they had hoped for, before a lot of the original people left the commune, was a giant "behavior laboratory." But that hadn't worked out, and now they settled on a lot of informal encounter groups, and on a once-a-week more elaborate session, called Encounter Night. We visited Encounter Night to see how the children fit into the main business of the urban commune.

Encounter Night was a version of the meetings that take place in every commune, when people get together to even scores and vent frustrations so they can stand each other for another week. It's amazing how many hours this activity took up, as many hours as most families spend in front of the television set. Here they had no television, and they didn't go to church, but Encounter was definitely a religious occasion, or as religious as you can get with urban psychologists who thought of divine revelation as a psychomotor deception. Here they had elevated the simple complaint to the level of mystical experience. Steve, who was Amy's husband and the prime mover of the commune, presided over the meeting, attended by all the children except Dixie, and by all the grownups. Steve was usually seen around the house, during the afternoons and evenings, wearing a conservative business suit which he called his "disguise" (but always managed to look very comfortable in). For these meetings, he took off the disguise and put on white guru robes and held a glittery cheerleader's baton called the Magic Stick. For a man with a balding head and a big nose and a successful paunch that dominated his five-foot-five frame, Steve managed to look less convincing in these guru clothes. Actually, he looked like Friar Tuck going off to meet the Maharaj Ji. Steve was in his glory at these meetings, standing over the rest who had brought the scruffy pillows in a circle around him. He flailed his arms around so dramatically that you could still see the Accutron watch ticking high up his arm.

You had to wait for the Magic Stick to be able to speak. It started to make the rounds among Donnie, Amy, Mary, Bill, Boog, Eloise, Mark, Michael, Jack, Karen, and the visitors. The children sat very attentively, like they understood the seriousness

66

of this event. They did not hold the baton, but just passed it along to the nearest grownup. We could not tell if they were allowed to speak. The children held onto and smoked the joints, which were flowing in the other direction. They were allowed to do that. The motto could have been: Children should be stoned and not heard.

The meeting progressed rather like a poker game. It started out with a few simple exchanges about the rules. Steve reminded everybody about the work board, said that nobody had signed up for weeding the garden, and that they might all have to do it over the weekend. Amy reminded everybody to pay his monthly food and rent bill. Donnie the nurse suggested that more people use the dental floss she copped from the hospital. Bill complained that the food buyer for the month (Mary) had been putting too much money into vegetables and not enough into desserts. He also accused unnamed people of having raided two chocolate cream pies in the middle of the night.

It was all impersonal, for a few rounds of the stick. But then people started the more direct attacks, and Amy and Boog and Steve and Mary and Donnie began to eye each other with a gambler's suspicion. Personal weaknesses came into play. Amy mentioned that Boog the carpenter, who had been hanging out here for two months, hadn't been doing his work. "I see vise grips on the table," she said. "I see wood and glue. But I don't see any work. And that's why we are paying your room and board." Boog the bulldog didn't let that pass. When the stick got around to him, he said he resented being a "slave laborer" during the day. "If I didn't have to open every stuck bottle and do half the work the women are supposed to do around here," he said, "I'd get a lot more shelves done." Mary said she resented that "stupid, chauvinistic remark" and then took the meeting into the thicket of high-stakes personal interplay. "While we're on the subject of Boog," she said, with offhanded amusement, "I don't like having a hard hat around here during the day. But what I really don't like is that he thinks commune women are an easy lay." That brought on some laughter. The psychologist, Bill, was the next to speak. In his driest clinical voice he suspected that

67

Mary was *flirting* with Boog, that Boog's "come-ons weren't all that self-generated." That remark made Mary mad. She said it was ridiculous. She also didn't like the "off-the-cuff psychological bullshit from somebody who isn't here most of the time."

Several such interchanges took place, beginning with a complaint and ending with an intervention from one of the psychologists. Bill and Steve would lay in wait for a certain level of irrationality, and then strike with clinical swiftness. That way, they were never on the defensive and always had the last word. But whatever Bill and Steve and the rest were doing, the children seemed to lose interest. They were no longer so attentive—Jack was petting a cat, Mark was carving a stick with a Swiss Army knife, Eloise was playing with a brainteaser puzzle on the floor—and the yelling and the accusations seemed to go right by them. A lot of what was said was remarkably childish for grownups who supposedly had been refining the art of living together. Mary called Donnie a "lousy cunt" for refusing to help her at the grocery store. But neither Mary's children nor Donnie's took special notice. The children seemed to accept verbal hostility like children of drunk parents accept drunkenness, or like the Latin Americans who can sit in outside cafes eating *cebiches* during violent palace revolts.

Sometime around 9 P.M., when the comments were getting trivial, one of the children finally took the stick. It was Karen, the dumpy black-haired girl with the American flag patch on her blue jeans. She opened up in an extremely loud and confident voice reminiscent of Jack's tetanus request—there were no verbally timid children here. "I want to say something about Amy," she said. "I think other people have noticed it, too. She's been real bossy lately. She hassles me about school, and does stuff like accidentally drop pans outside my room to wake me up. What are pans doing on the second floor?

"She knows school is my business. But she can't handle it. Just 'cause she's the oldest woman in the house, she still thinks she can tell everybody what to do. It's a big ego trip."

Karen's delivery was a little shrill, but it was effective. It was unusual to see a nine-year-old take on a grownup in an open field like this, especially when the grownup was her mother. Ben and LuAnne and Nina made their dissatisfaction known through their bad behavior, but they were not able to verbalize what was wrong. Those three had notions of their physical rights, but Karen was in there on another level of awareness, the level of emotional encroachments and what they might mean. She was aware of her mother's effect on her, of her mother's designs on her, in a way that made her seem much older than her nine years. It was somehow unsettling to witness that kind of awareness in a little kid.

It was also unsettling to Amy. She would deny it later, but you could see it in her face. She was trying to look impassive, in a Big Nurse sort of way, but she was failing. Her face was cocked. You could sense her mind behind it, all her years of wisdom, loading up with ammunition for a big volley back at Karen. She never got to retaliate, though, and the commune itself buffered what might have been the usual nuclear family reaction. Before Amy could get her hands on the stick, it went to Mary, who supported what Karen had said. That cooled Amy out considerably, and by the time she got to speak she managed to sound pleasant. "I know what the problem is," Amy said. "It's the big Jewish mother that captures me at night, when I'm in a weakened condition. When I get pushy, it's really her talking." It was the presence of the other people that gave Karen the impetus to criticize her mother in what seemed to be a constructive way.

The results of this meeting hinted at another possible advantage of communal life. It was a natural check on the invisible mother. Amy's meddling was not permitted by the group, or at least the group gave Karen a way to express her opposition to it. How many nine-year-old girls have that opportunity? Left alone in a house, Amy would not have let go of her anger long enough to hear what Karen had to say. And how did Karen even know what to say? It wasn't the freedom of speech that was impressive, it was a kind of emotional distance which allowed Karen to see her mother's faults clearly, see her mother as a person, unravel the mystery of her parents a little earlier than some of us who begin to do it when we go to college. Karen was the most tied to her parents of any of the children here. Maybe because she was the daughter of the only original married couple that still remained. She spent quite a lot of time with her mother, she did her homework, she went to school, and she carried on in many ways like she was still a part of a nuclear family. She had already picked up the psychological jargon of her father, Steve. She even looked like her parents—dumpy and fluttery. And yet she already had a clearly defined notion of her emotional rights, not just property rights, but her rights to be spared from the effects of her mother's admittedly neurotic behavior.

They all talked about their neurotic behavior. The children were therefore very aware of their parents' shortcomings, and had no illusions on that level. "If it wasn't for all of us," Mary said, "none of us would make it. We all have incredible blind spots that the others can see." The disadvantage was that they never stopped talking. Things never seemed to be worked out for certain. So after they got up in the morning, after the Encounter Night, Mary and Amy and Donnie and Eloise went over to a corner of the Cavern and rehashed the Encounter while they drank their coffee. Mary was giving a new analysis of the night's events with Karen: "The thing is, Amy, you come on as the villain, but it's not all your fault. Karen has a part in it too. I've noticed she hangs around you a lot, in the afternoons, and then when you get in too close to her, wham, she lets you have it. It's a game."

"We should talk to Karen about that," Amy said. "I think you're right." And so another discussion was created.

Then they discussed Jack's not talking to her mother Donnie. It was the celebrated topic of the week. "She's just trying to make you feel guilty," Eloise said to Donnie. "All this stomping around is just her way to get attention. She won't always be blaming you that way."

It was touching the way these people confided in each other, without a hint of the kind of defensiveness that Susan and her friend Margie exhibited every time they tried to discuss their children (they always came away mumbling that the other was "oversensitive"). Yet it was one of the reasons that the children seemed so bored during the day; all the grownups were too busy discussing how to improve their relations with children to spend much positive time with the children.

And sometimes, even with all the analyzing and planning that was going on all the time here, there were total freak-outs. One morning there was a major commotion down the hall, from one of the bedrooms that had no doors. It was a male voice saying, "Hey, kid, don't do that," with mild impatience at first, and then again, "Don't do that," now more threatening, and finally, "I'm going to kick that little bastard out in the hall." Then Mary said, "Don't be rough with him, he doesn't understand." Later we found out that Michael had gone in there to pull the covers off his mother's lover, a weekend visitor from somewhere. Mary tried to make light of it, but Michael appeared to be quite upset. He and Chauncey, who had played for several days without a problem, got into a fight and had to be separated. Michael, usually a cheery figure, sulked around, and periodically would run up to the male visitor and pretend to pinch him in the ass. The visitor, a man named Jeremy, pretended to swat Michael away like a mosquito, but you could see that Michael was perturbed. Mary said he had pulled the cover trick several times since she and her husband had broken up a year earlier.

Commune life had torn every one of these families apart. Maybe, as Mary suggested, they would have been torn up anyway, but in a place with no doors and walls and a belief in total openness, the children knew everything. No attempt was made to hide lovers or to soften the blows of divorce and attendant recriminations. Mark and Michael had arrived here with a mother and a stepfather, and they knew the ex-Hertz agent turned rock musician who had taken their mother away from their stepfather. They also knew each of the succession of lovers that their mother had since taken up with. Mark was even able to say, with some accuracy, that his mother had "the hottest pants in the commune." Michael could not be so jocular about it.

Karen still had her parents, but she knew that her father lived with another woman for a few months while her mother went to Europe for a vacation. And Jack blamed her mother's open

71

affair (it was with Bill) for the fact that her father had recently left the commune. Jack did not know when or if her father would be back.

Beneath these major breakups there had been a constant series of affairs and intrigues and subplots throughout the life of the commune. Amy said several of the original couples had left because they couldn't handle it. Mary, who was inclined to gossip in more specific terms, told us that Eloise had been a constant temptation to the "forty-year-old men who all have a thing for young girls." Eloise had made it with Bill and with Karen's father, so she covered both psychologists. Donnie, at one point, had taken up with Steve. Bill's wife had left the place with some other man, leaving Dixie behind. Mary alluded to several "relationships" she had gone through with different visitors.

They all talked about "relationships," not lovers, and they didn't have orgies or anything like that. Mary, for instance, saw her boyfriends not as a series of frivolous affairs, but as a series of potential lasting relationships that didn't work out. Couples breaking up every week, commotion in the night, jealousies galore, and yet Mary could still say, "We believe in the basic family unit. It's just hard work to keep it together." Actually, they loved the disruptions, the intrigues, and the chaos. It was all part of the behavior laboratory. As Amy told us, half-seriously, "Somebody has to break up every few days or else we wouldn't have anything left to talk about."

The line on the children was that since they had spent more of their lives in a communal place, they could handle the floating relationships and the disruptions better than the parents. It was part of a new notion of progress that they had, that Circle children would overcome some of the pettiness, some of the possessiveness, some of the ugly competitiveness, that the grownups carried here. It was hard to say. Karen, who liked to pretend she was still in suburbia, still had a childish faith that her parents could not be separated. She once confided to Susan that "they're older and they aren't so selfish." Mark, in contrast, had already developed a remarkably cynical attitude—he was always talking about who was fucking whom, about his mother's hot pants, about the girls he had fucked. An attitude reminiscent of Ben, except nobody around here paid any attention. They took it as one of Mark's poses, like his yoga routines. And Michael, too young to be articulate about it all, made his statement by pulling the covers off his mother's lovers. Once in a while he would talk about his daddy and speculate about when his father might come to visit. He said he didn't know exactly where his father lived.

Dixie also had her moments of petulance. She wasn't bad around Eloise, but usually ended up crying or throwing something when her father was around. He never spoke harshly to her or tried to correct her behavior. Mary said he still felt guilty about the mother's leaving.

Jack, of course, was still in full revolt, not speaking to her mother. It didn't seem that the children were handling the parental disruptions any better than the parents were.

How different were these Circle children who had emerged, three and a half years beforehand, from nuclear families? The commune certainly had not had a homogenizing effect on them, like what reportedly happened when the family structure was broken in China. They were all separate characters you could recognize in your own neighborhood—Jack the lanky, with her tendency to brood and make sour faces; Mark the social director, with his unchanneled energy; Karen the dumpy, who hid, behind the flaccidity of her body, a keen competitive drive; Michael the rough-and-tumble outdoors type. And the commune had not cut them off from certain aspects of Americana—they knew all the television shows. Even though the commune had no television set, they knew the Waltons, "Sesame Street," quiz programs. We asked Mark where he got this TV knowledge. Was there a kind of kid osmosis at work here? And he said, "Grandmother." That was another thing, the "grandmother factor." They all visited their grandmothers during the summer or for a week here and there, a week, Amy said, "of getting presents and being spoiled." It was a deliberate part of the training. "I don't want them to grow up not knowing about the kind of world we left behind," Amy said. "If they get a little of it now, maybe they won't go back to it."

73

How far were these children from the world their parents left behind? They had the communal house; it was like a Depression house with the extra people and commotion and mealtimes and the entertaining disorder of *You Can't Take It with You.* The house without walls gave them all a lesson in demythologication —there was no way to live in that place and come out of it honoring parents as parents, or sanctifying the Office of Parenthood. Jack, Eloise, Karen, Mark, Michael were too adept at psychological probing, too aware of the revealed foibles of their own parents to believe that parents are more than people.

The presence of other people also changed the lives of the children. The children lived in the paradoxical situation of tighter discipline and more independence. There were rules at the Circle, enforceable by anyone—rules against physical violence, deliberately trashing property, not doing chores, and so forth—the same behavior was expected of grownups and children. Penalties, meted out by the group, included missing a meal, or a kind of solitary confinement in one of the rooms. But mostly the discipline derived from an atmosphere of shared expectations, a lot of people believing and doing the same things.

The children's independence had nothing to do with rules or the absence of them—if anything, they had more responsibility than regular urban children. Ben's parents and LuAnne's parents had assumed that independence was a simple matter of abolishing a few rules. The Circle children had a kind of independence of spirit that derived from the presence of the group. Eloise, who said she had never gotten along with her real family, had in effect invented a new family at the Circle. She said living at the Circle improved her relationship with her mother, with whom she visited from time to time. Jack, when she was having particular trouble with Donnie, could find room here to stay away from her. Mark and Michael could spread their need for adult contact among a lot of people. There were no apparent sibling rivalries, possibly because every child knew a grownup who thought he or she was special. It was reminiscent of Aldous Huxley's *Island,* where every child had the right to choose his parents from the people he got along with best. "We scoff at arranged marriages,"

Amy said, "as being clumsy and cruel. But what about arranged childhoods? The way things are set up in most families, children never have the chance to know it can be any other way."

At the same time, there was a conspiratorial hush about the place which tended to isolate these children from the larger world around them. When Circle members did invite outsiders from the neighborhood, it was for symbolic exercises like the Race, which took place every couple of months. The Race was part of a day of games and activities in the backyard, when Steve was in his glory, walking around giving speeches on the virtues of group living.

The Race occurred when everybody lined up on a chalk marker, like they were ready for the hundred-yard dash, and Steve would shoot off a blank starter pistol, and the entire community would take off. They ran in circles, screaming wildly, over bushes and around trees, until they all fell down in mock exhaustion. Then they would line up and do it again, until nobody had the energy to get up. "There is no finish line in life," Steve was happy to point out to the onlookers, "and there is no finish line here. Everybody wins his own race."

They talked about living without competition, about how incompatible it was with communal spirit, and yet many of them were holding down competitive jobs on the outside. Steve, especially, was conscious of the irony, enough so that every time he came home from his office, he would throw down his coat, and declare, "That's the end of the bullshit for today, man." We asked him why he always had to say that, why he couldn't just come in and sit down. "I still have to work," he said, "but I want the children to know that I am just putting up with it. It isn't that I like to do it."

It took awhile to see through that fantasy, and what finally did it was Steve's studies. Steve, apparently, had been testing the kids all along, giving them the same psychological and intelligence batteries that most kids get in schools. He said he did them to prove to his own colleagues that the children had not been damaged by communal life, to encourage other parents to live this way. But I think Steve did the studies for his own benefit, to prove to himself that the kids were still bright. It was not achievement he cared about, but raw intelligence; he talked about the children's uniformly high IQs. He was one step away from the free school parents who worried about grades and permanent records; Steve didn't care about proving to the school system that the kids were achievers, he only wanted to reassure himself, on his own terms. And the children also talked about intelligence. Karen, especially, was always postulating that "that was an intelligent statement," or "that was a dumb statement." Mark, the least academic of all of them, introduced himself as the "smartest person in the commune." I think he might have doubted that; but one very conventional thing about all these children was that they were verbally aggressive and often snide. Snideness was not discouraged at the Circle; it was valued as proof of mental agility.

It was part of the confusion. Intellectual activity was valued here; it took up most of the adults' time, and talk put money on the table. Bill and Steve could come home and throw down their coats in a flourish, but it didn't hide the excitement on their faces when they discussed their work. The children knew all this; they heard Mary talk about the garden and about "self-sufficiency" but they didn't quite believe it. Eloise was totally committed to the commune; she had no desire to return to school. But the others, I think, saw through Steve's noncompetitive posture—they would be back in school next year. It was part of an unresolved drama of all urban communes: how can you let your kids drop out and still let your colleagues know they have 140 IQs?

The other confusion had to do with the role of the separate families in this communal place. Behind all the apparent open explorations of sexual relationships was the conventional belief in monogamy. The grownups were honest about it, of course, and honesty was a first step away from suburban hypocrisy, but they exaggerated the importance of that honesty in changing their children's attitudes about marriage and sex. Jack's protest against her mother and Michael's pulling covers off the lovers were classic examples of kids freaking out about a divorce or a separation—the extra honesty did not seem to have helped in those two situations. The kids did carry their parents' belief in families—Mark talked a lot about girlfriends, who his girlfriends were; Karen accused Jack of being too sullen to have boyfriends. There was no resolution, in urban communes, of the jealousy and loyalty questions plaguing many families. There was awareness, but no resolution.

It was impossible to predict if these children could go back to a regular house, or accept the change it would imply. It would certainly be difficult. They no longer accepted the role of being kept in the dark about things, or of being protected subordinates. As we saw in Jack, all these kids were willing to come out and deal with strange grownups on a person-to-person level. As we saw with Karen, all of them had been able to distance themselves from the neurotic incursions of parents.

Whether the effects of the Circle were exaggerated by the parents there, we were reminded of those effects at the end of our stay, when Mark said he wanted to go along with us for the rest of our trip. He wanted to see other communes, meet other people; part of it may have been his boredom in this isolated urban enclave. His mother said yes without hesitation. It was us —with the back of our car too filled with toys to handle another passenger, and with our reluctance to extend our parental responsibility—who ended up saying no.

At the bottom line, urban communes were composed of familiar urban professionals who had overcome a lot of the legal and possessive obstacles in sharing their children. And the children did not seem the worse for it. Being at the Circle was a challenge to a nuclear family, but in the rural communes we discovered people who were a lot more challenging than that.

4

Rural Communes

It is called the Ranch, a rural commune, a fairly typical hangout several miles up a dry gulch in a hippie-populated section of northern California. As in many communes, the Ranch had a splendid beginning. It was part of a worldwide LSD empire called the Brotherhood, an out-of-town retreat for people who made and sold acid for Timothy Leary. The land, several hundred acres of it, was paid for by Billy Mellon Hitchcock, a counterculture millionaire. The inhabitants included Nicky Sands, one of the premier LSD chemists, and several good friends of the Grateful Dead rock group.

But the days of high intrigue and publicity and big bankrolls from hippie millionaires have come to an end in the rural communes. In this particular case, according to an article in the *Village Voice* (by Mary Jo Warth, August 22, 1974), Billy Hitchcock turned in some of his friends, including Nicky Sands, to avoid a tax rap. By the time we got to the Ranch, Sands was in jail for making acid; he would later receive a fifteen-year sentence. Others involved in the acid empire are either in jail, in hiding, or dead. The only reminders of the old days are a 1919

Rolls-Royce station wagon, wood-paneled and looking very gangsterish, mysteriously hidden in the cow barn; and Ariel. Ariel is the five-year-old daughter of Nick Sands. She talks about him incessantly, writes him postcards, and occasionally visits him in jail. Every time the word "acid" comes into a conversation, Ariel perks up. She was standing in a restaurant when she heard a customer ask for antacid tablets. "My daddy's acid?" she gurgled hopefully. "This is one little girl who isn't afraid of her daddy's acid."

Like a lot of communes, the Ranch has become a loose and unpretentious place where people have enough energy to get the floor swept and milk the goats, and no larger purpose than getting through the day. The feeling of rebellion, and the companion feeling of paranoia on which many communes were founded, has disappeared. The neighbors are no longer horrified, and the reporters no longer come to write magazine articles about how this new civilization is doomed to failure. It is surprising how many rural communes are still thriving. Hundreds of people are together out here, in the mountains of New Mexico and Colorado, Virginia and the Ozarks and Vermont, Oregon and Washington, building independent water systems and mulching gardens, and getting along remarkably well with their straight rural neighbors. Communes are surviving, surviving on food stamps, gardens, frugality, group buying, bargain-hunting, odd jobs, bartering with other communes, hard work, salvage, and imagination. One thing has changed. There was a time when commune people had to defend themselves against those who predicted their demise. Now the position has reversed. After our trip, we began to believe they had a better chance than us.

Children abound in rural communes. The urban places often attracted older families and therefore older children who came from nuclear homes. The rural places are full of former teenage brides who had children when they came here; now the children are four or five or six. At the Ranch we discovered eight such children, ages six years down to eighteen months, who had known only a communal life.

79

The Ranch children are being brought up in relative isolation. The isolation is insured by an uninviting dirt road, full of potholes, that winds up the gorge from the main road to the houses at the top of a hill. There are no signposts on the road, and lots of possible wrong turns. Getting to a commune is always half the fun. You lose your oil pan, break your shocks, and get lost. If you are a tourist or an FBI agent looking for Patty Hearst, the commune is hoping you will turn back. We were about to do just that when we saw all the Ranch people working in the garden. About twenty naked farmers and their children, wallowing in fecundity.

The children were running around in between the irrigation troughs, throwing mud and making a general nuisance of themselves. Every few minutes an adult would yell at them to stop eating the big tomatoes, in a gruff "fuck you, kid" sort of voice. Immediately we were aware of two differences from urban communes—these children were not working and they were not treated "sensitively." Yet the gruffness did not seem to faze them. They kept on throwing mud and eating big tomatoes, and the adults kept yelling. Even though grownups outnumbered children two to one, it seemed like a rout in the other direction.

In scanning the garden, it was obvious who the real commune members were. The women and children. The men all looked pallid and sheepish, like they had just driven up from the Bay Area. The women were uniformly tanned and healthy and knew the answers to the men's questions, such as "Is this a weed?" All the men deferred to Jane, a skeletal woman with a Texas accent. It was a feminist's dream, seeing this slight woman explaining to three lumbering men how to fix the irrigation system.

The only permanent man in this commune turned out to be a former rock musician who came here with his two children after his wife decided she wasn't "into kids." The other men were either visitors, summer squatters, or part-time studs. It was a surprising fact of rural hangout communes that the original founders were men and women together, but then the men drifted away or went back to the cities or were arrested, and the nucleus of the commune, the solid core became the women and the children and the occasional single man with children. Men played a totally subordinate role in this community.

Susan and I were the only couple around this place. The rest of them had not only given up their original husbands or whoever the father of their children happened to be, they had given up the notion of a serious relationship with anybody—another difference from urban communes. Jane the Texan was Ariel's mother and Nick Sands's ex-girlfriend; she still liked Nicky and saw him in jail, but Sands had already married another woman while inside his cell. Jane's general attitude toward men was: "They're nice to see once in a while, but who needs them?" Alice, a tall red-haired woman, came here with Andrew and Annie, her two children, after she split with her husband. She thought he was in jail, but she wasn't even sure. She never saw him anymore and didn't seem that interested in talking about men. Josie was twenty-one and had a five-year-old son named Noah; she had occasional lovers but said she didn't get too serious about them. The same was true of Irma with her son Cato, Peggy with her daughter Joy, Leona with her daughter Liz. The last regular relationship to fail was Neva's, another twenty-one-year-old, with a child named Plum. Neva had recently broken up with her old man because, she said, "His planets weren't in the right places." Her attitude toward living with a man was "I'm glad that's over, now I can just be a person."

This man business might not have been so important, except that the lack of couples seemed to lead to an esprit de corps among the women here. The psychological skirmishes and complexities that took up so much time at the Cosmic Circle were not apparent. Josie told us that "couples are the enemy of communes."

The children were growing up without fathers. Except for Ariel and for Joy, they hardly even mentioned fathers. The men around them floated in and floated out. There has to be a new word for men like this; perhaps they should be called transparents. The idea of a permanent man was antiquated; the lack of one was no longer treated like a missing limb.

You have to see it to believe it. All the children stumbling out of the house before the mothers have begun to stir in their beds. It is not exactly the crack of dawn—the sun is already high in the California sky, browning the cattails, and the goats on the hill are complaining. It is the kind of farm where the goats are milked at ten-thirty, the cow (if she's lucky) at eleven. The theory going around is that animals can learn to get up later easier than people can learn to get up earlier. So far neither side has altered its schedule, and the children make preparations for the day without parental guidance.

The children get up earlier than most of the grownups, but they don't go to bed that much earlier. They wander through the evening as they please, listening to records, thumbing through comic books, making faces at the goldfish. They are allowed to fall asleep on their own sometime between ten and midnight, often dropping in their tracks as suddenly as pipeline workers overcome by gas. If their beds are near enough, and the children are small enough, their mothers carry them in. If not, they are awakened and made to walk to bed.

The beds are spread out among the three houses that make up the center of this commune—a large and once-fashionable big house, a white-shingled guest house, and a third cottage filled entirely with pillows, called the Zen House. There is total disagreement as to the best sleeping arrangements. Some of the children are still allowed to sleep in the same single beds with their mothers. Plum, Noah, and Cato are in that category, enjoying the pleasure of infants even though they are four, five, and six, respectively. The only reason their mothers give for letting them do this is that they (the mothers) like it. Actually, it is not surprising to see Plum in bed with his mother Neva, because even though he is four, he is tiny enough to pass for much younger. Some people say he is stunted because his mother is a fanatical vegetarian. We have seen her snatch hamburgers from his mouth and replace them with things like canned smoked oysters, and if anything would kill a kid's growth, it could be that. The other two children who sleep with their mothers, though, look much too big for this arrangement. Noah seems to be able to take or leave his mother's company; she often banishes him to another bed in favor of a lover, and without too much trouble. But Cato is so tied to the system that he spends between one and two hours a night arguing with his mother to come to bed early and not leave him alone.

Some of the other children are in a completely antithetical situation. They spend their nights in total isolation from their mothers. Andrew and Annie and Liz sleep in the Children's Room, a bunk-bed arrangement in the middle house, while their mothers are holed up in the woods in a tent. Ariel, an even more extreme case, is allowed to sleep wherever she happens to drop—in the porch chair, on a living-room couch—while her mother Jane is two miles back in her tent. If Jane was anything like Susan, she must have had to make a big adjustment to be able to fall asleep so far out of earshot from her five-year-old daughter. We found that out when we put Chauncey and Bernsie in the Children's Room and pitched our own tent back in the forest. Susan spent the first few nights at the Ranch stumbling through the forest, trying to sneak past a dread bull named Pickles, to check in on Chauncey and Berns—making sure they were still breathing. Bernsie was reaching out for Susan in her own neurotic way. She cried for several nights until informed that Susan couldn't possibly hear her (it was hard for Susan to admit she was actually out of Berns's range). Then Bernsie stopped. The other occupants of the room, Andrew and Annie (son and daughter of Alice) and Liz (daughter of Leona), never complained about spending the night so far from their mothers. They only complained that the room smelled like piss.

The remaining children at the Ranch did not fit either extreme category. Joy slept in the same room with her mother Peggy, but not in the same bed. And Pinky and Jeep, children of Bailey, occupied the floor of the Zen House while Bailey, their father, took the loft. Pinky was five, and she was expected to get her eighteen-month-old brother dressed and out the door without waking up Bailey. She already took many responsibilities of a grown-up mother.

The children emerge from the various rooms as disharmoniously as they were put away the night before. They collect themselves in the dusty driveway. On this particular day, Noah and Andrew have pants but no shirts; Cato has his hair combed and his hat perfectly placed on his head, but no pants. Joy is wearing shiny black patent leather shoes, but her skirt is on backwards. Pinky and Ariel have managed to put on clean dresses, but their faces are grimy, giving the appearance of coal miners who put on their meeting clothes without remembering to take a bath first.

There is something bizarre about them, milling around together before the breakfast gong is rung. It's not their general scruffiness or their runny noses (those are to be expected in a place like this), but that they have all tried to look respectable. Each of them has managed to do one thing. Andrew looks all right from the feet to the waist, Cato from the head to the neck. Maybe it was the beginning of a new communal spirit; as long as Joy brushed her teeth, it was good enough for all of them, and so on down to the shoes. Take a section from each Ranch child, and you have a single, well-dressed, clean, all-American child, who has done everything on the gold star checklist. Take them all together, and you have an incongruous bunch of ragamuffins. They looked like the *Lord of the Flies* children, trying hurriedly to piece themselves back together after spotting their parents approaching in the rescue boat.

Breakfast isn't any more civilized than they look. In most places, breakfast serves as a bridge between the primitive, subconscious dreamworld and hard realities of the day. It is the first chance for a parent to get at a kid and straighten him out, to cut through the rheumy haze with messages from the real world, like "Don't spill your orange juice" and "Sit up straight or you won't get any eggs." It is an educational opportunity and there is hardly a mother in America who fails to take advantage of it, promoting the Age of Reason and small motor control, along with the fried eggs. Breakfast can be a terrible time for a kid, but not at the Ranch. Like all the meals here, breakfast is not an excuse to mold behavior. Precisely the opposite. The way it works is this: two or three adults, the ones who have signed up for this chore, are huddled in the kitchen—two for cooking and one for beating away the attacking children who always try to sneak in and rip off a hunk of cake. The big table on the porch, where all the meals are served, is piled with a motley collection of plates and glasses—some plastic, some glass, some wood. The children troop in, scramble for a seat on the benches, and grab for their utensils. A large pot of oatmeal is brought in, ladled into the bowls, and then left on the table. The server retreats to the kitchen. The idea is to get out of the way before Noah turns over his milk, Pinky laughs at that and drools, Jeep bangs his spoon like a disgruntled convict, Joy starts to sing. The children scramble, they yell, they slobber, and they fight for seconds. It is amazing to see eighteen-month-old Jeep, already hardened from the food wars, rush the oatmeal pot, elbow off his competition, and serve himself with a long-handled wooden spoon. There is great determination on his face. He gets up on the table and rolls through the outstretched arms of the opposition like a diapered bowling ball.

These meals are always a free-for-all, and they are always fun. After they finish, the children pick up their plates (even Jeep), trudge into the kitchen to deposit them in the sink, and then leave the porch area in a uniformly good mood. The grownups reappear on the porch, like keepers after the animals have been let out, and wash down the porch with a broom and a hose. It was easier to turn on a hose than to convince a kid not to throw his food.

After breakfast, the children run up the hill toward the barn. It is now close to 10 A.M., time for Irma to milk the goats. The children always say they want to watch Irma milk the goats, and sometimes they say they want to help her milk the goats, but they never do. It just gives them an excuse to get up the hill. They travel in a mad pack. Andrew is at the front, he is the oldest (almost seven) and the heaviest, and he gets his way by bumping into the others with his beer belly. The others are close behind. Cato in his purple conductor's hat that he never takes off, Noah with a wary "Who's after me now?" look on his face, Ariel with that impish grin of hers, Joy with a stern dignified walk that makes her look like she is in a processional, Pinky and

Liz and Jeep. Jeep is struggling to keep up, moving on tiny fat legs against the giant diapers that seem to cover half his body. The only absence from the pack is Plum, who is back in the house arguing with his mother over what he ate for breakfast.

From Susan's point of view, this trek to the barn is a catalog of dangers. She is worried about Chauncey and Berns, who have lost their clothes, lost their patina, and are covered with dirt and berry juice like the rest of the children. It is the first time this commune trip has gotten to her on a gut level. She is worried about the general surroundings, which include old refrigerators, rusty nails, long sharp metal bars, old hammers, rocks, disabled cars, and Pickles the bull. She is worried not about the surroundings per se, but about the fact that six- and five- and four- and three-year-olds are allowed to scramble through them with the same lack of parental guidance they receive at breakfast.

Pickles is always at the top of the hill, waiting for the children. Cato plays bullfighter and taunts him with his purple hat, waving it in Pickles' face and making loud groaning noises. The bull looks bewildered, like he can't decide whether to sneer or to charge. Only a few inches separate his horns from six-year-old Cato.

It's like that at every turn, a matter of inches. Joshua has a long metal pipe in his hand swinging it in a wide arc that just brushes by Pinky's ear. He isn't trying to wound her, he just doesn't see her. Chauncey hurls a wooden spear that sails a few feet to the left of Jeep's eye. Andrew is wrestling with Noah, slips and topples back on a rock, bellowing like a wounded moose. Annie is bumped by Joy and runs behind a tree, falls down, and pretends to faint. Annie always does that when things get out of control. The Ranch mothers, in the only instance they used psychological language to describe anything, said that three-year-old Annie is "catatonic."

Not knowing about Annie's tricks, I run over to pick her up off the ground and find her laughing at me. Every ten minutes there is a near miss of some kind, or what appears to be a breakdown on the part of one of the children. It is impossible to watch them without cringing.

The mothers aren't watching. That's what happened to us after a while; there was too much open space, too many children to monitor, too many potential problems, so we just stayed in the house with the other grownups. The mothers took the morning hours to do their chores, cleaning and washing, and so on. Their main concern about the children, at this point in the day, was keeping them away from the back porch.

I tried to tell Susan the difference between her and these other mothers was trust; they trusted their children more than she trusted Chauncey and Bernsie, and trust creates trustworthy children. But it didn't turn out to be true. Jane and Alice and Josie, the most articulate of the women, were full of stories about how Noah tried to burn down a tent, or Andrew cut the water hose with an ax, or Ariel tried to tie the goat's udders with rubber bands. They referred to their children as "mischievous little fuckers" or "conniving little bastards" so often that we realized trust didn't enter into it. At the urban communes, the line had been, "If a kid is responsible, he can have his freedom." Here they could have their freedom anyway.

The Ranch mothers were philosophically detached, like mothers who have already gone through ten children and dozens of broken arms. And yet they were very young—Neva was twenty-one and looked fifteen, Josie was twenty-one; Irma, twenty-three; Alice, twenty-seven; and the senior mother, Jane, was only now approaching thirty. Maybe because of all the astrology charts in the house, they believed that whatever happened would happen anyway. A kind of Latin-American fatalism. Jane said they had given up on the idea that you could create a safe environment, an idea on which Ralph Nader rests his case. So they were going in the opposite direction from flameproof sleepwear and childproof aspirin bottles and around-the-clock vigilance. Jane also said the communal accident rate was a lot lower than the accident rate for children in the cities, where the mothers worry more.

We couldn't prove that or disprove it, but we saw no serious accidents. All the children returned from the hill with their limbs and eyes intact, enough days in a row so that Susan began to relax. There was no other choice, really. Just as they did not enter the breakfast room, these mothers did not choose to fight the battles of civilization on the level of dirt and scratches. Dirty kids, bruised kids, a missed meal, a few days without clean teeth, late nights, rough-and-tumble antics were all accepted. The Cosmic Circle children had been on their own in the emotional and verbal conflicts of the day. These children, much younger, were on their own on a physical, survival level.

The pack had its own way of handling things. The children got along with each other up on the hill; we saw no overt acts of hostility or premeditated hatred in our entire month at the Ranch. When Annie went limp, the other children would ignore her. When Andrew moose-bellowed, he was likewise ignored. When Noah demanded to be the mother in "Mother, may I?" the others wouldn't play with him until he recanted his dictatorial attitude. There was very little resort to the Big Guns; hardly ever did a child threaten to get his mother. When they were hurt, they worked it out themselves. Not all to the same degree—Andrew had a habit of seeking out his mother, but Jeep was truly remarkable in his ability to withstand pain. Often stung by wasps, Jeep would go over by himself, sit down under a tree and cry until the hurt left. He did not call for Bailey. Anything less than a wasp sting, and he wouldn't even cry. The only other thing that brought on the tears was when he couldn't reach the serving bowl for seconds of spaghetti.

This formless running around did not hold the children for the entire day. The pack would get tired of Pickles, tired of the junk pile, and return from the hill—sometime around eleven-thirty. They seemed to reach out for some order in their lives. Noah suggests some group games, but always with the intent of being the leader; Andrew accuses him of trying to run things, and the games dissolve. Joy, who often acts like the most grown-up of the children with her snippy, fastidious manner, offers "Button, Button," and the kids get excited, until nobody remembers how to play. It is impossible for this group of children, who roam so well together, to do anything that involves structure or reason. They turn to food and sex. Ariel takes one group on a foray into the basement to get the bananas. They are stopped at the cellar door by Bailey, who clucks, "You know better than that." Andrew leads another group to the children's room for what they all call "breeding." Andrew, the principal breeder, gets up on the bed with Pinky, while Annie guards the door.

The mothers joke about why the children think they must guard the door. Whatever breeding entails to a six-year-old, it doesn't bother the mothers. Sex interests the children for about ten minutes. After that, there is nothing left to do. Now the children turn to grownups for help, and it is obvious why they have not learned to organize group games. The grownups can't organize anything, either. In fact, there is nothing separating children and grownups, in terms of the magic and formlessness of each day. None of the adults has a regular job, none of them even has a watch. They get their chores done, but that's about all. Additional projects have a way of not being finished. Jane and Susan wanted to get together on making some sandpaper letters, to begin to teach the children to read. But with all the confusion around here, they never got beyond the letter *c,* and the sandpaper and glue were left in the garage.

The children wait, like hitchhikers, around the dirt driveway that circles the house. They know if they wait long enough, something will happen. Jane decides to go downtown to check the mail; she picks up the nearest four children, shoves them into the back of her Toyota, and takes off. She promises candy. The remaining children return to waiting. Alice decides to go for a swim in the nearby lake. She grabs a few more children and stuffs them in the old Chevy. Noah and Pinky and Plum, the only remaining children, don't take any more chances. They get into the jeep, knowing that sooner or later somebody will be going someplace. Soon enough, Bailey decides to drive to a neighboring commune to pick up a visitor. That takes care of the early afternoon. The children will all pick up an apple somewhere for lunch.

No wonder these children always seem to have a mystified look on their faces. They are swept up by events. Nothing is ever planned for them. Nothing can be. An entire rock group arrives from San Francisco, and the afternoon is transformed into a raucous maelstrom. Visitors appear and disappear in literal droves, visitors from other communes, old friends, people who have heard about the place. There is always room for one more person at the table here. A truck driver named Al periodically appears out of nowhere to take one of the children on a trip. He tells Andrew to pack his pillowcase, they're going to Los Angeles. Within minutes, Andrew is on the road, gone for six days.

Even the taking of baths, which usually involves some coaxing and preparation in regular households, is handled by blitzkrieg at the Ranch. Any time a grownup is on the way to the shower he picks up the nearest child, strips him down, and drags him in. In this informal fashion, the kids got clean at least every couple of weeks.

Susan said that since the children had no appointments, they had no disappointments. It was true; since there was no buildup for anything, no looking forward, the children were not too upset when things didn't happen. There was a day when Neva wrote on the message board (everybody's way of keeping up with things) that a rodeo was being held in a nearby town. The mothers had a short discussion about it, and decided to go. They shoved all the kids into the three cars and started down the hill. One of the cars broke down—they always did in communes, children did not expect an eventless ride anywhere—and they left it by the side of the road, squeezing the extra people in the other two cars. That made about twenty people in two cars. After a sticky and uncomfortable hour's ride, and plenty of jostling and bickering among the children, they arrived at the rodeo. It was an empty parking lot. A man circling around on a motorcycle said the rodeo was next week. When the Ranch people tried to match up with the world's plans, they got it wrong more than half the time.

Some children are told about the Thanksgiving Day parade and *told* about the Thanksgiving Day parade, and if the car breaks down on the way or something, they can get very unsettled. Not these children. They made fusses about other things, like Noah's complaining that Andrew was jabbing him in the stomach, and Joy's demanding that Pinky quit pinching her ears. But as to the rodeo, they just accepted the empty lot and tried to work with that. Andrew told the man on the motorcycle he wanted a ride (these kids were as forward with adults as the Cosmic Circle kids) and the man said OK. All the children got rides and came home satisfied. I heard Ariel recount the story to somebody who hadn't gone. She talked about the man on the motorcycle, but she didn't even mention the rodeo.

You would think, since there were no music lessons or base-ball practices or after-school plays, no apparent planning for children on the part of the grownups, that the Ranch mothers were exempted from the drudgery of raising kids. They wanted you to believe that, Josie and the rest of them; Josie was always talking about how "we don't take any shit from the kids here." But there was no way to believe it during an afternoon at the Ranch. The afternoon was when things invariably broke down.

The people are back from the beach or from town, the chil-dren are tired of running around outside, and the grownups are tired of guarding the kitchen. The children close in on the house, making smaller and smaller circles, like a strangler vine. In a minute, they seem to be everywhere they are not supposed to be. Ariel has made it to the pantry and back out with a cookie, prompting more to try. Noah pulls a comic book off his mother's lap on the living-room couch, to complain that Ariel got a cookie, why couldn't he have one? He is kicked out of the house through the porch entrance, but comes in again through the kitchen and tries Alice with the same complaint. She gives him a cookie. Andrew, meanwhile, has decided he doesn't like the music; he pulls the needle off the record with a screech that means the record is ruined. Jane grabs him and throws him off the porch for "trashing." He gets up, comes to the other side of the house, and asks Bailey if he can go in the living room to watch the goldfish. (The goldfish tank, incidentally, is very near the record player.) Bailey says yes, Andrew returns trium-phantly to the scene of the crime and stands there, daring Jane to throw him out again. Jane doesn't even notice; she is busy with Ariel, who has stuck her thumb into all three of the pies. Ariel is an adorable troublemaker who can crinkle her nose in a way that makes you laugh while you are spanking her.

The parents talked tough to the children, but no question of discipline was ever permanently resolved. Peggy could tell Ariel to keep out of the pie at 3 P.M., but it didn't apply to three-fifteen, when Ariel was back again, doing the same thing. Only one of the children, Liz, had a reasonable ability to listen to instructions. It was no accident that we hardly ever noticed Liz, and didn't discover for two weeks that Leona was her mother. She was invisible in the pack of clever, demanding, and in their own way, obstinate young disrupters.

I think the children knew how to use the confusion of this place to their best advantage. First of all, each of them had a completely different defense to adult pressure. Andrew, when thwarted, would moose-bellow until the grownup in question gave in to guilt. Annie would go limp in your hands, until you gave in to fear. Ariel put on her impish grin. Noah lobotomized himself, pretending not to understand and saying "huh" to all contrary instructions. Plum was so small, and so victimized by his vegetarian mother, that he got away with a lot on compassion alone. Joy adopted a dramatic Gone with the Wind posture. Pinky pouted and acted bitchy. Cato whined and hung around.

By late afternoon, all the kids were using all their tricks and the effect was hectic. Even in a one-on-one situation some of the mothers were outmatched with their own children; Cato, for instance, could always get the best of his mother, Irma. But in a group situation, all the mothers were outmatched. The kids would go from one grownup to the other until they got what they wanted. Nobody remembered who had said what to which kid, or which kid had been asked to do what five minutes ago. And the kids knew, instinctively, which mothers were most susceptible to their particular brand of persuasion. Jane fell for antics and funny faces, Josie gave in to a kid who would pretend to listen to her tough talk, and so on. We could see why the Cosmic Circle mothers had needed so many meetings to continue to present a united front to the children. Here they only had one meeting a week and it was not usually to discuss children. Children were hardly ever discussed, and chaos was the result. The trashing and badgering and yelling continued into the evening.

Susan, who grew tired of all this commotion, especially around dinnertime, suggested that children and adults have separate meals from each other. As it was, they all ate together in a scene that was pretty much like breakfast. But surprisingly enough, the mothers *liked* the commotion and the presence of the children; they tried a separate meal for a couple of evenings, then went back to the old way. They wanted the communion of all the people jumbled into the main house together, even if the price was constant hysteria. It stayed hysterical until the kids fell down sleeping, but there was a lot of amusement in the process.

One thing the Ranch children thought about all day was food. It was true of the children of many rural communes. Poverty wasn't the reason; the Ranch people were surviving very well on welfare, windfalls, the garden, odd jobs, and one person's investment income. There were plenty of groceries in the larder, and yet the impression was of always-foraging children. The only game that got the children together was hitting the larder. An adult was literally on duty all day somewhere near the kitchen, holding the children back.

The food rumor hotline was always on with these children. We made the mistake, in the beginning, of offering one or two of them a package of apple-cinnamon oatmeal from the back of our car. The others were playing up the hill, far out of sight, and yet in a matter of hours every one of them had come back to touch us for his package, until we had none left.

We had taught Chauncey and Bernsie that they could eat whenever they were hungry, as long as it was healthy food, that speaking up for what they wanted was a good thing to do. Here we cringed when they asked for something, knowing that eight other requests would follow. So we ended up teaching them conspiratorial silence—if you want something, just give a wink, we'll take you outside, and you whisper what it is. A very anticommunal attitude.

For the rest of the children, the food frenzy occurred not because of what they ate, but how. Dinner might be served anywhere from 5 to 11 P.M., depending on who was cooking. On certain occasions, it might not get served. A pot of spaghetti might be attacked by twenty people, or if ten visitors magically showed up the moment it was put on the table, thirty people. (It always happened in communes—extra people coming from nowhere when the food popped out.) The children were used to this situation, as they were used to chaos in all phases of their lives, and they sensed the general precariousness of their position. So they stored up when they could, like winter animals. No mealtime routine had dulled them into a false sense of security; they were perhaps the first unpoor Americans who did not think of food as a matter of divine right.

Competition was part of it, too. You could tell that by Jeep, who always huddled close to the serving bowl and was ready with his spoon the minute the bowl hit the table. They said they were against competition here, and it's true, there were no races or awards for achievement, and yet whatever the children didn't get from not hearing about Vince Lombardi, they got at the dinner table. Sometimes it was children against children; sometimes, parents against children; sometimes, parents against parents, for that slice of apple pie. One night Susan and I brought some pizzas in from town and the kids sneaked into the kitchen and gobbled them before the grownups knew what was happening. The next night Irma made apple pies, and the grownups retaliated by barricading the kitchen door and eating up the pies before the children even heard about them. Fifteen grownups, sitting on the floor of the kitchen, gobbling goodies and guarding the door. It was a major triumph. Josie couldn't resist telling some of the kids, "Ha, ha, you little bastards, we had pie and you didn't."

Susan and I smoothed over the problem of communal fairness versus individual appetite by taking Chauncey and Berns on frequent trips to the local restaurant. It wasn't exactly fair, but that's the only way we could handle it: having at least one or two meals a week where you didn't have to wonder if the people next to you would take your share of the seconds. We also began the subversive practice of taking Chauncey and Bernsie up the hill, slipping them an apple or extra piece of candy, and ordering them not to tell. "If you tell, that's the end of the snacks." They caught on fast. It was the first time Bernsie could keep anything quiet.

For some reason, Susan had the courage to admit our sins in a group meeting toward the end of our stay. She told Jane and the rest about our sneaking the candy. To our total surprise, Jane and Josie admitted they did the same thing. All the mothers had been up there, meeting their kids behind trees and rocks, and slipping them candy bars, but nobody had been talking about it.

The other area of constant concern, besides food, was disease. It was no accident that when asked what sicknesses he had heard of, Noah rattled off "strep, hep, syph, and clap." Strep, hep, syph, and clap, plus colds, crabs, gono, and mono were the scourges of communes. The kids knew about all of them. If the regulars weren't sick, there was always a visitor to infect them. At the Ranch, for instance, the infectious visitor was me. I had come down with a bad case of hepatitis from another commune in Colorado, arrived here, and promptly turned yellow. I was treated to a level of kindness and tolerance that I would never have extended to somebody who contaminated me. Nobody at the Ranch blamed me for polluting their commune, or grilled me on how I possibly could have contracted such a dirty disease; they just turned up the heat on the dishwasher.

Peggy, the mother of Joy and the most traditionally concerned of all the mothers, spent a lot of time with a communicable disease manual in her hand. If it wasn't hepatitis, it was somebody with strange spots or green skin, or weird-looking bumps on the neck. We took the children swimming in a river that we later found out had been condemned. That brought out the book; Jane spent the morning reading about the dread diseases of bad river water. It was a game they played—match the symptoms with all the possible diseases. Nothing was ruled out—a bump on the neck might be the beginning of mumps, of viral pneumonia, or the earliest signs of the bubonic plague.

Every day there was a major freak-out, something that threw the entire commune into mass hysteria. Often these freak-outs had to do with disease. Rumors of a new one could sweep through the place like smallpox used to sweep through primitive island tribes—and everybody would go momentarily crazy.

It happened one morning, when people trudged routinely into the porch and the kitchen. They saw a note taped to the refrigerator. It read like this: "Congratulations, folks, you've got it. Nancy [a child who had visited here for two days] has been diagnosed with typhoid. Remember typhoid? Maybe not, it is a rare disease. Remember Typhoid Mary? There is a long and glorious history to this one. Almost wiped out, except for around here. But we have it, and it is contagious and sometimes fatal. Look it up in the book, you'll be amazed. Cheers. Henry."

Henry is a local hippie entrepreneur who sleeps here sometimes, and his reputation for reliability is low. But nobody considered the source, and this little note jolted everybody. Neva, the vegetarian mother, went into a total fury, giving a speech next to the refrigerator about how awful this place is, all the dirt and sloppiness, how everybody uses the same toothbrushes and lets the kids run around and expose their tender bodies to danger and sickness. It was a farewell speech. "We don't give a shit about our kids," she said. "I've had it. I'm leaving." And she disappeared to pack her bags. Nobody knows how to deal with Neva when she gets mad like this. Peggy went to find the book, to look up typhoid. The others tried to remember what they could from old high school history and hygiene courses. Jane suggested that Typhoid Mary hung out in the Orient. Josie wondered if there isn't some kind of vaccine, "or is that only *before* you get it?" Alice tried to remember Nancy's visit, if any of the kids kissed her or breeded with her. Nobody seemed to know. Jane smiled and suggested mass suicide. Irma wondered if the animals could get it.

Everybody was in a rotten mood. Except for the children, of course, who witness one of these frenzies almost every day. They just stood around dumbfounded while the stew increased with each new person coming in and reading the note, being shocked, and telling what *he* remembered about typhoid. Henry, the original source, wasn't around.

Out of twenty people giving their opinions, nobody suggested going to town to ask the doctor. There was no way to call because there is no phone here, but town is not more than fifteen minutes away. I was going in anyway, for my hepatitis exam, so I told everybody I would stop by. Nobody thought it was a worthwhile idea. Jane said one of the doctors was good, but he was on vacation, and the one who remained was an "asshole."

I found the asshole doctor and asked him. He looked totally confused. He said yes, he examined Nancy and that she had a cold, not typhoid. He said there hadn't been any typhoid recorded in this part of the country for several years.

When I brought back the good news (and complained that they made me look like a fool), the major upheaval that had been taking place immediately subsided. Too quickly, I thought. Everybody had been eager to analyze the situation when the place was seething with myth, rumor, and hysteria, but now that true facts were known, people got bored. Jane said it was another "failure of communication." Alice complained about Henry: "How can you trust a Gemini?" Neva unpacked her bags and returned to dancing to the Grateful Dead.

It was the kind of major scare that would have had the Cosmic Circle people mulching for weeks. What about what Neva had said in her fit of anger, about the dirt and the lax policy on visitors, and the dangers that the children were routinely exposed to? She said, "Aw, I was just pissed off." Now that they were off the hook on typhoid, she would save that speech for the next panic.

All the mothers were like that. They didn't fight disease in the calm periods between the freak-outs, and they didn't fight it on the first line of defense—dirt and grime and mouth odors and harmful bacteria. They were motivated only at the point of hysteria. The prospect of a grand calamity like typhoid interested them, but the prospect of cleaning up didn't.

There is a point to be made about the health of these children. They didn't look well cared for, on a superficial level. On three occasions, we talked to doctors who treated commune children, and also had worked in urban areas. All three of them said the same thing: commune kids are uniformly stronger and healthier than suburban kids or city kids. It must have taken a lot of convincing evidence for them to say that—all three were straight doctors in their late fifties who believed in washing hands and brushing teeth and changing clothes every day. One of the doctors, who lived in Denver, was the father of a commune woman, and he wasn't too pleased about how she was living. Yet he was emphatic about the commune's effect on children. He said the diseases that commune kids pick up are the old-fashioned ones, easily diagnosed and easily cured. Diseases that the rest of us have learned to avoid and therefore can be properly outraged about. But new diseases, caused by poor diets and chemical additives in food and water, the commune children do not have. "If it's a choice between an obvious case of strep or a hidden case of lung disease," he said, "the kid with the strep is better off."

The great typhoid incident solidified the impression that these people didn't think like we did. It was hard to pinpoint the difference at first—Jane was a college graduate and Josie and Neva and the rest were high school graduates and we all had read the same history books and spoke roughly the same language. But one began to sense, in talking to them, that they had given up on logical thought. The psychological realm so present in the urban communes had disappeared, and in its place they put the stars. Jane didn't get along with Steve because he was a Virgo and she was a Taurus. Henry was unreliable because he was a Gemini. Even the animals, whom they talked about more than the children, were ornery or complaisant because they were Libras or Capricorns or Tauruses. Astrology was the end of every discussion. You would gab around some subject, like why the mothers were so susceptible to rumors and notes on the refrigerator, until somebody mentioned the sign, and that was enough. It signaled a change of topic. Life could not be explained; it all came from the Great Horoscope Writer in the Sky.

The books that filled their shelves, alongside the ever-present Meher Baba poster ("Don't Worry—Be Happy"), the flowering plants filling one wall of the living room, the constant odor of incense, were all about the unexplainable, the *I Ching,* astrology, a smattering of Zen, yoga, ESP, witchcraft, and black magic. Or else they were about simple and practical things—how to garden, how to can tomatoes, how to shoe a horse. That's how their minds worked; they had severed the cord between the practical and the mystical, a cord on which the whole American dream of progress is transmitted. They seemed to have primitivized themselves, to see each moment as wholly separate from the next. The note on the refrigerator was a downer, and the good news from the doctor was an upper, but as for the reasons behind the downer or the upper, nobody really cared.

The children were a little young to have their thinking analyzed, but we noticed a few things about it. For one, their misbehavior wasn't based on deliberate calculation, it's just that nothing was ever explained to them. Noah put his hand in the cake, and Josie would say, "You little bastard, get out of the house before I knock your head off," but she never told him *why* he shouldn't put his hands in the cake. There was no appeal to reason, which is why the mothers had to say things over and over. The children remained in a perpetual state of savage innocence, and it was part of their charm—nothing they ever did appeared to be premeditated.

We never got to see the Ranch children alone, because they were never alone. They all knew our names immediately (which I found surprising), they were aware of adults as real people and not just as people who had come to visit their parents. They were totally warm and friendly and at home with the idea of strangers; there was no getting-used-to period that you sometimes have to overcome with young kids. But they stuck together, always. They were hardly ever alone with us, and hardly ever alone with their own parents. When the pack ran it was difficult to pick yours out, and we had to stop trying.

We could sense the effects of this kind of life in what happened to Chauncey. Susan lost control of him for the first time. She got very uncomfortable about it. We did see him around the house during the afternoon, but he wasn't reachable, available for talks and for working things out. Susan had always been able to talk to him, but the lines were down. Chauncey had also taken to swinging sticks and acting very pushy. He questioned our authority in a way he never had before.

The same influence was good for Bernsie, who could not cling to Susan here. She stretched her rope more than ever before, sleeping with the other children, running with the pack. She even gave all her clothes away. It was the first place she had been where nobody called her pretty, or adorable, or commented on her dresses, so I guess she knew the dresses were useless. She was also much less bitchy without her clothes on.

After a while, we lost our inhibitions about the Ranch. The dangers were here, and the haphazardness, but there was something about the scene that we trusted; the people got along quite well and they cared about each other in a way that had not been true of the Cosmic Circle people. Susan and I left for a couple of weeks, while I recuperated from the hepatitis, and Chauncey stayed behind at the Ranch with a paper bag full of clothes. Just like a commune kid. He wasn't returned to us on the appointed day, which freaked Susan out totally; she had visions of him impaled on the horns of Pickles. But we got him back in one piece a few days later.

In return for taking Chauncey, we invited Andrew back to the little resort where we were staying. It gave us a chance to see him outside the community. Andrew had lived in two or three communes with his sister Annie and his mother Alice, before they had settled on the Ranch and remained there for about two years. Andrew was almost seven, a heavy redhead with a beer belly and a truck-driver way of talking.

There were other children running around this resort, and we expected that Andrew, who was accustomed to lots of children, would help push Chauncey into this new group. We figured Andrew to be naturally gregarious, but it wasn't true. Andrew turned out to be shy and reticent; Chauncey contacted the other kids, but neither Andrew nor Chauncey made much of an effort. They hung around our little cottage, just like they did at the Ranch, asking for snacks and waiting for us to do something. Andrew seemed despondent and listless without the ready-made gaggle of his friends; the groupism didn't carry over for him. He was a much more energetic and adventuresome child on the hill of the Ranch than out here on his own. He seemed as dependent on that group as most children are on their mothers.

We got along quite well with Andrew, except when we took a grownups' prerogative and said no to him. Susan and I wanted to watch television in our bedroom one night, while the children were in the other bedroom. Andrew couldn't understand that. Not the television part of it; he understood television, although the one at the Ranch was in the basement and hardly anybody ever watched it. But the separation. He complained and we sent him outside. He bellowed like a moose for over an hour. I got mad at him, until I realized that he had never been deliberately segregated from grownups before; at the Ranch there was no activity (except staying in the kitchen) that the children couldn't share with the adults. It was touching to think of it—children and grownups in one big happy family—but we kicked him out of the room anyway. Andrew also wasn't used to taking orders. He squabbled whenever we told him to do anything.

We returned to the Ranch with Andrew, and he immediately perked up and became cheerful. It was so apparent that he was tied to the Ranch; if the other children were like him, how would they handle school? The end of our visit was also the end of summer. Andrew and Joy were six years old; most of the others were five—the kindergarten age. It brought on the inevitable debate—except here the question was not about education—it was if getting up at six is worth the advantage of being free of the kids for the rest of the day. The mothers agreed it was at least a possibility—they were going to try it.

Seeing the Ranch prepare for the school year was like seeing Indians get transplanted. A simple thing like public school, which is established for the convenience of the parents, was a total mystery to these people. Josie was worried that the children, being used to an open bathroom door, wouldn't understand the thing about "boy" and "girl" and why the division was necessary. Jane thought they wouldn't be able to stand in line, after all the meals on the porch. But these potential adjustment

101

problems were nothing compared to what the parents had to face. They had to face getting up earlier than the goat.

Somebody gave Peggy two alarm clocks. Being the most responsible, she was elected to try and wake the rest. The required school forms were sitting on the porch table, waiting to be filled out, but nobody filled them. They were thrown out with the trash.

The morning of school. The clocks didn't go off. The children got dressed and woke up the parents. Andrew didn't have shoes on; he never wore them. Jane and Alice scoured the houses and came up with one boot and one sneaker. He had to wear the mixed pair. Ariel had no blouse; she borrowed one of Bernsie's out of the car. Noah demanded breakfast. Peggy gave them each a carrot and a piece of halvah, the only stuff around.

They were supposed to have name tags, but nobody could find paper to write them on. They ended up writing on paper towels. The commotion kept up until somebody reminded Jane it was getting late. The preparations ceased, and Jane grabbed a few kids and dragged them toward the jeep. The jeep wouldn't start, so they all piled out and got into the Toyota. For all the extra attention, the children managed to look the same as usual—some of them were dirty, most of them were uncombed, and Ariel still had red war paint on her forehead.

As the car headed down the mountain toward the bus stop you got the feeling that this experiment would never work out. The transition was too difficult. The mountain commune, and the life it supported, was not translatable into the public schools as the life of the urban commune children had been. There were hardly any links to the outside world. These parents didn't hold on to any notions of intellectual achievement, they truly didn't care about that. They also didn't seem to be so mixed up about couples and families. There was no double standard in the rural communes, there was a totally separate standard. The young products of that standard gave off a much different feeling than the urban children. Even at their tender ages, you could tell they were different. The Ranch children were beautiful, disorganized, and friendly. They lacked an urban aggressive edge; they were neither calculating nor hostile. The lack of hostility was amazing; they approached adults and each other with an openness we had not encountered before. They were happy on the mountain, in their group, and on the mountain their lives made sense.

But one could not help wondering what would happen to them. Most of the rural children were quite young, of course, too young for us to question their future. That future, in great part, depended on how well the commune parents could perpetuate this separate society; and nobody knew the answer to that. It was enough to say that the young children were thriving in their present situation. We decided to look for some older kids to see how this movement was preparing to perpetuate itself.

❧5❧

A New Civilization

We met Andy Peyote hitchhiking into Taos, New Mexico. Just one teenager with a backpack, strung along the road between young mothers breast-feeding their babies while simultaneously waving their thumbs at passing pickup trucks. There is one of them, a teenager or a mother, about every tenth of a mile on the roads around Taos, studding the dust-bowl terrain like living billboards. It seemed like incredible luck, given all the available riders, for us to have picked up this particular child. From the minute he sat down in the car, Andy Peyote let us know—with the pride of somebody who has a senator for a father—that he was the son of Mickey Peyote, a legendary figure in the New Mexico and Colorado mountains and the founder of two communes. Mickey Peyote was right at the top of our list of people to see, but we worried about even getting into his The Last Resort commune, which had a reputation for friendliness akin to that of a western gunslinger town. And here on a Taos road, roughly

150 miles to the south of The Last Resort commune, we had already captured his son.

Elated by this fortuitous quirk, we were also immediately confused. "How old are you?" we asked. "Twelve," the boy in the back seat said. "Then what are you doing down here if your father is up there?" "I don't live with my father all the time," he said. "Your mother?" "No, not while she is with Mr. Dolan. He's the meanest man in the valley." It turned out that Andy Peyote was sharing a trailer in back of the goat pen at the Taos Learning Center with another twelve-year-old, named Tim. We had heard of the Learning Center before—a teenage commune-school that we had hoped to visit. This single hitchhiker had given us a direct link to two places, and possibly more.

Andy Peyote said he was going into Taos to buy bullets, so he could "shoot some rabbits for protein." Not meat, mind you, but protein; one way to tell the alternative hunters is that they don't shoot animals, they shoot minimum daily requirements. Andy Peyote spoke with drama, like if he didn't get those bullets to shoot that protein, then he would die of starvation. He didn't look at all desperate, though; he had puffy chipmunk cheeks and plenty of meat on his twelve-year-old body, and the kind of cherubic twinkle in his eye not seen on most faces of people who are struggling for survival. He said he existed mostly on the recipients of his bullets, plus a few staples bought with food stamps; and yet nothing about him, from his cowboy shirt down to his work boots, supported his presentation as a young Daniel Boone on welfare.

From the first, this pioneer Peyote treated us with a "yes, ma'am" sort of deference that fit the innocence of his face much better than the details of his story; he acted like the best-behaved child we had ever met. I say "acted" because we weren't sure, at first, whether to believe him or not—he immediately took it upon himself to stop Chauncey and Bernsie from bickering (they had been doing a lot of that lately) by telling them stories of his pet rat Ponderosa and then sitting between them so they couldn't torment each other. It seemed like much too helpful a role for a twelve-year-old hitchhiker, especially one who lived on his own and killed for food. It was such an anomaly, the coincidence of picking him up and then the emergence of this courteous, cadet-like child, directing us through hippie Marlboro country, with mountains on all sides and dust engulfing the pickup trucks, and the people on the road looking like the cast of *Easy Rider*.

There were a lot of communes around this area, but from Andy Peyote one got an immediate sense of being inside a vast network. Every place we mentioned, he had lived or worked, or recently spent the night; he seemed to know all the people. Lama, yes, he had just been up at Lama for their Sunday visiting day, and a Sufi master was giving religious dancing lessons. Reality, yes, he was just over there, and did we know they were tearing Reality down, brick by brick, and carrying it over to the Magic Tortoise? Commune adobe was around like the Italian marble in war-zone churches; as one place falls they pick up the handmade adobe bricks and take them to another. Andy Peyote said he was considering living at the Magic Tortoise, when they finished it, so he could be near a friend named Mike. New Buffalo, he knew all the people at New Buffalo; "It's right across the valley from the Taos Learning Center"; and he said that two children we had hoped to see there, children who supposedly burned the place down, no longer lived at the commune. He had a direct line on the most recent happenings at all the places—hepatitis at the Red Rockers, Morningstar going out of business, a new baby at The Last Resort (where his father lived)—and yet the communes he was describing had no telephones and were spread out over 150 miles of mostly impassable mountains. It was a first inkling of how interconnected these places had become.

In Taos, we waited while our prey bought his groceries. He returned to the car with the bullets, and with a bag of rice, and three candy bars, two for Chauncey and Bernsie; the other he ate and then carefully stuffed the wrapper between the seats of our car. His roommate Tim would get "pissed," he said, if he knew about the candy; he was only supposed to buy food. Today was. his turn to buy, Tim's turn to cook. "Too bad for me," he said, " 'cause Tim is a lousy cook."

The Taos Learning Center turned out to be an adobe house, a couple of trailers, and several Indian teepees scattered around a completely treeless plateau about twenty miles out of town. With an outdoor kitchen consisting of charcoal-blackened pots stacked behind a vinyl plastic lean-to flapping in the breeze, the Learning Center was a dead ringer for an abandoned prospector's camp.

Andy invited us into his trailer, just behind the goat pen. It was as close as you could ever come to a twelve-year-old's paradise. Blankets falling off the bunk beds, war comic books strewn all over the floor, unwashed pots clogged with uneaten rice and beans drifting in old water in the small kitchen sink. Cartridge boxes for tables, fishing rods hung on the walls, several guns placed around the room. If you looked carefully at the guns, you noticed that two or three of them were real and the rest were toys. The young hunters hadn't shot an animal all summer. They used their bullets on targets and cans, and their protein came from food cooked in the communal kitchen. Guns had nothing to do with their survival; guns were props for the elaborate war games that Andy played with his twelve-year-old roommate Tim —two boys camping out on the far edges of their fantasies, without a parent to pull them back. Tim was usually wearing a World War I gas mask, and he circled around like a disabled plane. We hardly ever saw his face, we just knew him as two eyes inlaid in a metal canister. I don't think he took the thing off, even to brush his teeth.

Five or six teenagers were living at the Center, all about the same age as Andy. It was hard to tell whether this was a school or a commune. They called it a school, and yet only a small shelfful of books, lost in the surrounding horse blankets and guitars and sleeping bags that filled the adobe house, reminded one of traditional education. It was the middle of the summer when Andy brought us here, and yet the students were still living in their trailers or their teepees, in the exhilaration of teenagers freed of their parents. Marian and Luna, two fourteen-year-olds, shared a stooped-over Okie truck with a cedar shingle roof. Both of them had been here for more than a year, away from their mothers, who they said they didn't particularly get along with. Luna called the Taos Learning Center her "home."

At first the Taos Learning Center seemed like an older and more sophisticated version of the Ranch—a lot of people floating through, chaotic mealtimes, prevalent astrology talk, kids roaming around on their own. The primitive dangers that first disturbed us at the Ranch, the rocks and sticks, gave way here to more developed hazards like guns and hitchhiking and the bottle of LSD cooling in the refrigerator—an unmarked jug of drug abuse sitting right next to the Borden's. It was no different from being with most teenagers with growing access to drugs and cars and sex, and all the things that parents worry are happening behind their backs, except that here everything was out in the open. The only adults around, except for floaters, were Tom and Aline, a trippy couple in their middle thirties who had given over their own house to the Learning Center and moved into a teepee on the back ridge.

It was hard to tell, in the long run, how these teenagers could handle this freedom and their opportunity to live alone. Andy Peyote seemed responsible enough, with occasional lapses into childishness with his friend Tim—all of the kids were going through that transitional stage when they had discovered the heavy trips of sex and marijuana and travel, but were still equally turned on to candy and movies and playing war. The striking thing was how unimportant these freedom issues were, ultimately, to either Andy Peyote or the grownups who lived here. It was the middle of the summer, the usual time for teenagers to exercise their independence, but the teenagers here appeared to be involved with something else besides pitting their will to experience against a parental will to repress. They were working to keep the Taos Learning Center alive and solvent.

This place began as an experiment by a man named John Kimmey. He didn't actually live here, but he came over to visit every couple of days. Kimmey, a robust man in his middle thirties who people might confuse with Jim Kiick, the football player, arrived in Taos through, he liked to say, "elimination." He started out as a regular public school teacher, and then abandoned that as ridiculous. He started a free school in Santa Fe, and then saw—as we had seen—that free schools didn't seem to be leading anywhere. So he moved to Taos with the same notions as many of the commune people and commune sympathizers that populated the area.

Kimmey thought that if the alternative society was to survive, then you had to train alternative people. You couldn't just rely on the isolated communes, stuck away from each other in the mountains, to perpetuate themselves and stave off the system. You had to somehow unite them in knowledge and in manpower. So he set up a school, which could draw on all the young people in the valley, on a voluntary basis. They would have to live here, as a commune, and learn to survive on their wits. There was no tuition at Taos Learning Center, no salaries, and most important, no budget. If the school was to survive, Andy Peyote and the other twelve- to fourteen-year-olds who chose to live here had to think up ways to make money, or barter, or grow food, or something. The school and the community were the same thing. "We don't want to put out people who go to Pittsburgh to become computer programmers," Kimmey said. "We want people to learn how to survive right where they are and stay together where they are." It was, to the hippies, what a prep school is to a rich family, a chance to learn the skills that keep their people alive. The skills, of course, were different—instead of getting grades and learning to compete and calculate and work for personal rewards, these teenagers were supposedly learning how to cash food stamps, how to cook, how to make adobe bricks, how to scam and get good junk parts and exist on their wits. The incentives were entirely patriotic—there were no grades, no payments, no benefits except the chance to live here in autonomy from grownups.

The students came and went freely from the Taos Learning Center and back to their communes or to their homes. During the regular school year, Kimmey said, the place attracted more people. Even so, his dream of an alternative civilization seemed a little grandiose to be supported by five or six or even ten students and a few adults and an adobe house—but on a personal level it had a powerful effect on these particular young people. In spite of the fact that it was summer, and there was marijuana in the cabinet and movies in town and kid action everywhere—and no grownups who told them what not to do—Marian and Luna and Tim and Andy were up on the ridge, stomping adobe bricks. Every day. Well, to be totally truthful, Marian and Luna were always stomping bricks; Tim and Andy arrived a little late and left a little early, but even they got in a few hours a day. Stomping adobe, we found out in our five minutes of participation, is no joke. It is hard, sweaty work. They were doing it, they said, because the school had agreed to make Tom and Aline a new house in return for the one they had donated. A new house was the schoolwork for the year. It was also the basis for whatever formal training took place—in building it, they learned brick-making from a local old-timer (that was another Kimmey notion: get the old-timers to teach the young hippies), and they learned geometry while measuring angles for the foundation. We, too, forgot the dangers and diversions and got caught up in this project, at least from the standpoint of admiring it. The project seemed to be all the discipline the students needed.

It's hard to tell what practical stuff had rubbed off on them, but in their struggle for survival they had developed an extraordinary sense of communion. Maybe it had to do with the equal freedoms, and with Aline's remarkable attitude for a house-mother: "The best way to see if your kid can handle the acid you know he's taking is to take it with him." Or maybe it was the shared sense of purpose. Or maybe it was just being in the mountains, but there was a definite religious aura about this place. We all took a sauna together, crushed up against one another inside a small hole in the ground that looked like a bomb shelter, all naked and sweating and chanting and saying prayers. The teenagers were in there, and the adults and the visitors; the thing I remember the most through the heat rising and the people chanting and hugging each other is that there was nothing between us. It was a group sauna they had every week to re-enforce their solidarity, really, but the solidarity had to be there already for everybody to get so naked and so close and still feel so good. I tried to imagine what it would have taken to get my high school teachers together with the students, naked in this hot little clay room and with their arms around each other. Or my parents in there with me. Or a building contractor in there with his customers and his workers. All of these relationships were part of the people at the Taos Learning Center, and yet they were all somehow overcome symbolically in the sauna and actually in the daily life. It's another thing the teenagers were learning—how to be close to each other, in a communion of spirit, in a way that I, at least, had never before experienced.

But solidarity or no solidarity, Andy Peyote was anxious to move on. You could see the conflicts in his face—he wanted to stick around for the adobe project, and also to make $150 to pay the teacher of a mind control course. Apparently that's what twelve-year-olds did around here, take mind control courses instead of buying bicycles. He owed the money, but the responsibility of the debt paled against the prospect of seeing his father at The Last Resort. Temptation overcame him; he said he could make the money back later. He showed up at our tent with his rat Ponderosa and a big wooden cage and his sleeping bag, and said he was taking us up on our offer to drive him to The Last Resort. I got a kick out of this twelve-year-old's mobility. He could apparently decide, on the spur of the moment, to pick up and go anywhere. He never had to ask his mother, who lived only about ten miles away from the Learning Center. Here he was traveling with two total strangers (four if you count Chauncey and Bernsie) and yet there was no need, he said, for us to stop by his mother's house to be checked out. The Houston murders were in the paper that very same week, grisly stories about boys Andy's age who disappeared from home and turned up as bodies a few months later. "Do you always take rides?" we asked him. "Not always," he said. "It's a thing you learn. My father told me to look into people's eyes. That way, you can tell if they are crazy or not." He seemed very sure of himself—at least, it's a better way to decide than looking at people's clothes.

So our eyes checked out and he shared a ride with us. Not, though, with the certainty of a boarding school boy who is going home to see his father and knows he will be let in the front door. Andy Peyote was unsure of his welcome; he hadn't seen Mickey in over a year, and he was wondering if Mickey's girlfriend Sarah would forbid him to enter the house because of the pet rat Ponderosa, Andy's prized possession. If it was a choice between staying with Mickey and Sarah, or staying with Ponderosa, there was no question but that Andy would choose the rat. The rat, in fact, was running through hoops he made with his fingers while he mulled over the possibilities. "If Sarah doesn't want me," he finally said, "there are a lot of other people at The Last Resort that do." He saw himself, it seemed, as a child of the whole valley, and it gave him a powerful sense of security. He looked forward to everything with a sense of adventure that reminded me of the Ranch, actually; he did not expect plans to work out. His life, he said, was "a trip."

Out of the way of Tim and his buzzing airplane noises, Andy reverted to the state in which we had originally met him—polite mediator for Chauncey and Bernsie, eager storyteller, cherubic and acquiescent, intent on answering all our questions. A small alarm bell in the back of my head told me he was conning us, especially when we stopped in a Mexican restaurant for lunch, and sensing that we would pay for him, proceeded to order the most expensive things on the menu and gobble them up. Like he didn't know when another chance like this would ever come along again. But we returned to the car and he charmed us out of all our doubts by telling the children a story from a book called *The Borrowers* about little elves who lived in a basement and borrowed things from the people upstairs. It seemed like too quaint a tale for a budding Tom Sawyer.

Andy Peyote guided us through about thirty-five miles of unmarked dirt roads after we got off the highway. We could never have found The Last Resort without him; it was at the end of the last dirt road on the side of a mountain, bordering the national forests. And his hope of acceptance turned out to be entirely true—as we drove up into the parking lot (containing eight or nine old cars) beside the machine shop, everybody ran over to greet him and hug him and pet his rat.

112

The Last Resort was built by liberal-arts-college graduates. It was impressive how they had gotten this place together. They had the snow-capped mountains and fresh mountain streams and verdant forests and rolling meadows to work with, of course, so that gave them an advantage—a lot of beautiful land donated by a hippie millionaire. Most of them had migrated to The Last Resort five or six years ago from an earlier commune called Drop City, a pioneer commune, a dome place blessed by Buckminster Fuller that dissolved in bickering and one murder. Since that time they decided that the bad vibes of Drop City were irrevocable; some of them returned to the straight life, others came here. Not to make the same mistakes, they decided to hide their houses so they couldn't get too close to one another; there was a rule that no house could be in view of another. That contributed to the beauty of the place, which was a genteel beauty, more like a golf course condominium than like what we had seen in Taos.

They build it all themselves, a dozen or more homes from trash and scrap lumber, and how-to-build-a-dome books and a few hundred dollars. Nobody was an architect and nobody was a carpenter. It wouldn't have been so impressive, had these been simple shack domiciles, but they were *Better Homes and Gardens* inlaid-wood specials, perched on the tops of mountains, constructed around giant boulders with an engineering intricacy and polished exactitude that you don't see much anymore. Carl the oil painter, Marge his potter girlfriend, Mickey Peyote, Sarah the former Houston debutante, people who looked and talked just like their friends who went to graduate school, had put this place together. Not only the houses but everything else. They had learned to fix their own cars. More than change the oil and plugs, but rebuild engines. While we were there a woman named Pat broke out, shook down, and rebuilt an entire jeep, part by part. They had also devised their own water system, using the mountain streams; maintained a gigantic garden; milked goats every day; dug elaborate latrines; and delivered their own babies. The results of five years of experimentation were more than just a few funky cabins and people adjusting to a rough life. The Last Resort, notwithstanding its tough cowboy image

113

(which its people liked to cultivate as protection), was the Darien executive's dream of dewy forests, swooshing fountains, sculptures on the lawn, elegant domes with sun porches, and women walking around in old cocktail dresses—what he might hope for in retirement after twenty-five or thirty years of commuting. Here they had managed to do it without waiting—just on trash and scraps and leftovers and zero net incomes.

Andy Peyote was at home at The Last Resort from the moment he arrived. He and Mickey Peyote looked exactly alike: two tall, skinny, grasshopper people with mischievous twinkles in their eyes. Imagine you and your father running away from home together and you get an idea of their relationship. They pursued the same fantasies—although Mickey must have been in his late thirties—off to hunt a deer in the woods, or to hitchhike down to Mexico, to run after some caravan of nomads rumored to be in the area. Mickey Peyote loved to tell stories of outlaws and of his own illegal adventures, and made a point of shunning the outhouse and shitting next to a flower every morning. That's the kind of man he was. He would emerge from a perfectly ordered dome, kept that way by his compulsive housekeeper girlfriend Sarah, and roam the woods until he found the right flower. He shit with the same mystical care that Don Juan hunted.

So we could see where Andy Peyote got his adventure and wild West spirit, his fantasy about shooting rabbits to keep alive. It was interesting to hear the things that he and Mickey talked about, usually over a hash pipe at the dining-room table. Legends mostly, but they had nothing to do with hard work or Horatio Alger or what made America great. They were all stories about the forces beyond man's control—evil spirits, twists of fate, Jorge Luis Borges, Indian legends and visitations, death and cosmic retribution behind every tree. Instead of minimizing life's dangers or throwing out a life raft in his stories, Mickey Peyote took great delight in glorifying them to his son and to everybody else. He was the most eloquent spokesman for a feeling that you get in almost all of the communes, of astrology and mysticism and a return to a more primitive flow of life. Children like Andy Peyote and the Ranch children are growing up in this philosophy. Everybody else outside of communes seems to be on that technological life raft where things might get safer and safer, until pretty soon Ralph Nader is running the life raft and things are safest of all. The Peyotes are down there in the river and they come on fearless.

The Last Resort people tried, within their suburban setting, to live the life of the natural man. People didn't always trust each other, a fact attributed to the distance between the houses just as the violence at Drop City had been attributed to the closeness of the houses. The mistrust often led to fights, but instead of decrying the fights, The Last Resort people seemed to glory in these periodic explosions of anger. It was part of the Peyote philosophy of natural, violent, and unpredictable nature. "The guy who owns the bar in town," Mickey told me one day in front of his sprinkler system, "said that the thing about hippies is that they have no self-control." He was very proud of that.

There were several fights—a woman named Lillian spent the night with Mickey Peyote and her boyfriend Dave got mad and trashed their house and threw spaghetti all over the walls. It took two days to clean up. Mickey's girlfriend Sarah had a full-blown tantrum with Jack the mechanic; she screamed at him for more than a half hour while he was trying to lift a car out of a ditch with a derrick truck. She was hissing and scratching at him while a two-thousand-pound car dangled precariously over their heads; it was a straitjacket-level display of anger. A few minutes after that, Mickey squared off with Jack, both of them crouching around the water tank and swinging metal bars and threatening to bash each other's head in. Finally they gave up growling and went home.

The actual violent part of Mickey Peyote the natural man didn't seem to affect Andy Peyote. He was quiet and mild-mannered, and he never raised his voice. The other children, too, never fought among themselves; they seemed to handle the commune better than the grownups. But we did see one result of the mistrust; Andy Peyote, an essentially communal child, did not have great faith in communes per se. He kept warning us not to lend our car to other Last Resort people, "or else it'll end up in a ditch." His security seemed not to be in the future of The Last Resort, or any single place, but in floating between them and among them and surviving on his own.

The relationship between Mickey and Andy is fascinating because there were no years of education or training or growing up required for the twelve-year-old to exist on the same level as the thirty-five-year-old. No guardianship on Mickey's side, no adolescent contortions on Andy's side. They did things together, not as father and son, but truly as people. They could go out to shoot deer, to take peyote with the Indians, to scam for valuable junk, to order books from the Book-of-the-Month Club under fictitious names, without any apparent hard edges separating one from the other. Like the sauna. I could see in my relationship to Chauncey something very different already coming through—Chauncey is a child who loves people and adventure and yet I am always dissatisfied with how he ties his shoes or why he can't ride a bicycle. "You should know better than that," I always say to him, measuring him against the mythical *you* who thrives on such comparisons. It has to do with expectations. Andy Peyote seemed free of any expectations as far as his father was concerned, as far as anybody who hung around him was concerned.

I don't know how it had been in the earlier years, when Andy lived with his mother and Mickey Peyote, or even how it was when the couple split up and Andy moved with his mother to Taos. But at the age of twelve, he seemed to have endless options—he played life in a very wide ball park. At The Last Resort he appeared in several antithetical roles. Sarah fell off a loft and hurt her back (refusing to go to the hospital) and Andy stayed in the house and did the dishes and cooked and kept up Sarah's share of the garden, all without complaint, like a perfectly domesticated child. The week after that, when Sarah was back on her feet, Andy ran off with the Coyotes, a local teenage gang that hides out in the woods and apparently survives on robbery and on shooting sparrows. He stayed with them for several days, out in the woods, then returned to The Last Resort and announced he was going to live with the Red Rockers for a while. The Rockers were all sons and daughters of Beverly Hills movie stars who stayed together inside a mammoth sixty-foot dome and powered their record player with a windmill. Andy's flexibility was amazing. He appeared totally unconcerned with what The Last Resort people would think of his being a part-time Coyote, or conversely, what the Coyotes would think of his being a part-time mother's helper and houseboy.

But what was to become of Andy Peyote? He crystallized the trepidations about commune children. The other children were running chaotically through the domes at The Last Resort just as they had run at the Ranch, but they were younger, and maybe because of that, we didn't take their situation seriously. We had met two children back in Taos, the two who admitted burning the entire New Buffalo commune to the ground when they were five years old, and now they were in public high school and playing basketball and going to church and leading a completely conventional life. So we could see that there was time for things to happen, for parents to return to the straight world, and for children to return with them. But Andy Peyote was twelve, and approaching the age when kids begin to sift through careers and search for the thing they can do best, a specialty to build a life on. He was as intelligent and gifted and experienced as any twelve-year-old could be and he seemed relaxed and happy in his world of scams and trips and mobility, but for some reason we could not keep him there, in our minds. We wondered if there was still time for him to hitch a ride with the real world, if there was still a chance. We tended, actually, to judge all commune children that way: Do they still have a choice? meaning, Can they still get back in?

The question came up the first night we had dinner with Mickey and Sarah in their dome, the Scarsdale of the dropouts. Sarah was outside, to direct Chauncey and Bernsie not to step on her petunias and her begonias, and then inside to direct them not to sit on certain pillows and couches. It was an impeccable dome, really, a showcase dome—and the walls were lined with the same books Susan and I had read in college. We even spent a few minutes identifying the courses—English 101 in one corner, Anthro 10 in the other. Mickey and Sarah were just like urban professionals, in the sense that they built a hedge of their education. And while we were on the subject, I asked Andy Peyote if he ever wanted to go to college. He hesitated, and before he could answer, Mickey said, "That's bullshit." "Yeah," said Sarah, "bullshit." Andy, of course, then said no.

School was a constant issue, and beyond John Kimmey's limited attempt, we had seen no viable plan of any commune to create one. Many commune people started with good intentions, but then inertia and just keeping alive would take over, so they would end up sending the kids to a public school in which they did not believe, or else let them stay at home and run around. So naturally, we got very excited when we heard that a woman from a commune near The Last Resort called Mañanitas was planning to open a school to serve the children from all the communes in the area. That included The Last Resort, where seven or eight children lived; the Red Rockers; the AAA, home for a rock band of the same name; and Mañanitas itself, a large farm which shared its produce with all the other communes.

We went to see Rosalie, the woman who was planning to turn her own two-room house into the educational center for the valley. We even offered to help. "Far out," she said. "You got a VW wagon, right? Well, then you can be the school bus."

It sounded like she was ready to open the school in a matter of days, and we visited all the other communes to map out our bus route on all these impossible dirt roads. We returned to The Last Resort to wait for the announcement of the beginning of classes.

A week went by, and two weeks, and still we had received no word. We got a little skeptical, and went back to visit Rosalie again. "Just when will this school start?" we asked. "Oh, I don't know," she said, in that vague communal way that makes you feel like a fascist for even looking at a watch. "Whenever it gets together. Maybe by the solstice." I couldn't even remember what a solstice was.

Just at the point that we doubted if we would ever hear from Rosalie again, we got the news that a fence-building party was being held at Mañanitas. A fence for the school. It was just an extension of our disappointment—here was a woman who had never taught school, had no certificate, no books, no paper or pencils, not even a bathroom in the building, and the most pressing need she can think of is a fence. But all The Last Resort people were invited, and we wanted to see Andy Peyote in as many different situations as possible. So we went.

We arrived at Mañanitas Farm at noon, when the work party was supposed to start. A few people were wandering around in a haze. Somebody picked up a fence-pole digger, but it didn't work because it needed a bolt. They searched around half-heartedly for a bolt, but none could be found. Somebody else tried to start a gas-powered saw, but it wasn't sharpened. They looked for a sharpener but couldn't find one. "Is there a shovel around?" a man yelled out. No shovel. "That's it," he said. "We tried. Only thing to do is roll a joint." So we sat up on the big pile of uncut logs in front of Rosalie's house and smoked a few joints.

What a typical hippie project, we thought, an extension of the chaos we encountered in every communal place. No tools, no schedule, people talking about "getting it together," standing around and wasting their time. I felt sorry for John Kimmey, when his dream and his adobe-hardened teenagers came up against the slumpiness of the movement. But nobody else seemed concerned; there were five or six long-haired people in bib overalls laughing with Rosalie, who had appeared from her house to see how things were going.

We were about to leave when the trucks started coming over the hill. Two hours late. There were about ten of them, old Chevys and Fords with bald tires and doors hung on with rope and bailing wire. Rosalie stood up on top of the woodpile and yelled out names like she was calling the horses on the far turn: "Here comes the Red Rockers, and there's the AAA, and there's The Last Resort." There was a general air of excitement. People piled out of the trucks, more people dressed in bib overalls and heavy woolen shirts and carrying simple tools. The women had long dresses and babies on their backs in papoose carriers. From the other side of the property a woman wearing a filthy leather smock and Indian shoes rode up on a white horse. It was Su, a Chinese doctor who used to practice medicine in California, but then dropped out and came to Colorado to ride around on her horse and deliver babies and make free communal house calls. A total abandonment of professional bearing; there were no M.D. signs on her horse, nothing about her suggested that she wanted any recognition for all those years of medical school. She even volunteered to do menial work.

Susan and Su went into the house to cook spaghetti for what was now a crowd of more than fifty people. It looked like what the movies call an old American barn-raising, children playing together on the grass while their parents laughed and drank from a big communal waterbucket and worked up a good sweat. It was the raw will of fifty stoned people battling against general incompetence and rusty tools, a mythic struggle between the hopes of a new society and the requirements of an old one. In about four hours, the raw will won out. With a few old saws and shovels and fifty uncoordinated workers, a beautiful hardwood fence was circling the school on three sides, for a distance of about three hundred yards. Everybody got into a giant circle and held hands, and looked at each other like they didn't believe it. Rosalie was beaming, she got in the center of the ring to announce that "this place got very high today," which was true.

After we broke hands, the kids ran toward the pot of spaghetti —like the Ranch children they were taking no chances with food. By the time the rest of us walked over, most of it was gone, but nobody seemed to care. A man named Dulcimer Dan, who we had already met back in Taos, showed up with his musical instruments, and there was an instant dance that lasted into the night.

Most children in America haven't seen anything built by a minga of neighbors, all getting together without the attraction of pay. It was quite inspiring, actually, to see how much could be done. Mickey Peyote and Andy Peyote were right in there with the sawers and hammerers, and after the dance, I said to them, "If you could only harness that energy, ten minutes' worth from every commuter in Grand Central, you could probably build a better Grand Central in less than a year." "Who wants one?"

Andy Peyote said. Now that he wasn't riding in our car, he no longer treated us with so much deference.

We went back the following day to Mañanitas, and Rosalie was cleaning up the paper cups and the spaghetti stains on her walls. She said that now that they had a fence, she was sure the school could start in the next week. "What are you going to teach?" Susan asked. "I haven't got that together yet," Rosalie said, "although my sister is coming down here. She used to teach retarded kids in New Jersey, so she must know something. Got any ideas?" Chauncey suggested duck-duck-goose, a game he liked to play, and we left it at that.

Everyone ended up satisfied with this school that had one out-house for thirty children, and took care of health problems by insisting on one paper cup per child, and solved the academic questions with a single book, called *What to Do on a Rainy Day*. Just another free school. After about a week of classes, we heard that Rosalie wanted to shut the place down for an indeterminate period. She was worried the health authorities would discover the school on a rumored spot-check of conditions in the communes. She knew they would demand certifications and flush toilets and a regulation kitchen and a lot of other stuff that could never be handled here. For a few days, Rosalie wanted to pretend that the school didn't exist—that it was just a house. A funny house for a twenty-five-year-old woman, with pictures of elephants and giraffes on the walls, but the health authorities think hippies are crazy, anyway. When the coast was clear, she was going to send out the word that the kids could return—like the people in the back room of a Prohibition speakeasy.

But after this school expedition, we changed our attitude on the whole matter. We had gone to see a school get built, and returned not thinking a school was that important. It was the fence party that did it, seeing all of the people work together like that—it was our first inkling of how narrow and constricted our notion of education had been. In looking for a classroom, we had not paid attention to the remarkable education going on around us. We began to think of Andy Peyote's life as valid on its own terms—valid and full and, in a way, enviable.

A few days after the fence-building, Andy Peyote went out to fix the water system, which had broken down somewhere between the mountain stream and the Peyotes' dome. As he began to patch the hole in the pipe, it appeared that everything in the commune world was in the control of the people. They talked about mysticism and fate and stuff like that, but when it got down to what they put into their mouths and what they breathed and how their society was organized, their system was a lot more graspable than ours. They had taken their water back from the city control boards and all those agencies that the rest of us must rely on, in primitive faith. And they didn't call the city to fix the pipes. A twelve-year-old could do it; he could follow the line right from the house to the source.

At every level, life was like that. Almost the antithesis of the educational process that prepares people for a specialty. Andy Peyote had a completely different mental world from our children—he believed he could make a life out of spare parts and his own head and the spur of the moment. He had seen a fence built that way, he had seen communities built that way.

There was always a project. After the fence, it was bringing a six-thousand-gallon water tank up the mountain, for a reserve water system. Andy was involved on every level. He and Mickey drove off for two days to negotiate with several towns to get a used tank. They finally found one, and spent another day haggling over the price. Then they talked somebody into lending them a truck to bring the tank to The Last Resort, on the condition that they could put a new clutch in the truck. So they discovered a mechanic in another town who sold them a used clutch cheap, brought it back to the truck, pulled the old clutch, and inserted the new one. They returned with the truck to pick up the tank, found some holes in the tank, and patched the holes. The rig was loaded, and about twenty miles from The Last Resort, the truck developed carburetor trouble. So they spent the night in the cab of the truck, then hitched back to The Last Resort the next day to borrow the commune's rainbow-painted flatbed, to pull the other truck. After several minor breakdowns, they managed to get both trucks up the mountain. By this time, the other

Last Resort people had dug a concrete foundation for the tank, and a few of us got together to set this gargantuan metal container into place. The truck almost turned over from the weight of the tank, and as it was swinging over our heads, I thought of how many experts this project would have employed back in Miami. And how much it would have cost. And how Andy Peyote would never have been allowed to go along, for insurance reasons. How he would have been told, "Leave it to the experts, we know what's best."

I thought of our own house, and the parade of tilers, plumbers, roofers, and bug specialists that came through almost every week. The Last Resort people were not only fixing things, they were helping develop a philosophy of the world for the children who watched them. Chauncey and Bernsie already knew that we didn't trust our own opinions about leaks, sicknesses, and termites, and that the working of every life-support system from food to water to shelter was a matter beyond our control. It already affected their views on occupations. I was putting up a shelf and Chauncey said, "You can't do that. You're not a worker."

You could say that Andy Peyote was just developing a country handy-andy ability, but that didn't explain everything, because even the American country children are now growing up in a mysterious world of experts. Not skilled people, but experts. There is a difference—The Last Resort people had skills, but they didn't act like those skills were beyond the ability or understanding of the other people who didn't have them. Everything was an occasion to learn. A girl named Lillian had her baby at The Last Resort while we were visiting, a time for the entire community to watch. Andy and all of the younger children gathered around the bed. No question about how this baby got from its mother's stomach into the little crib behind a glass case at the hospital, no need for the books that ask, "Where do you come from?" The doctor arrived on her white horse, dressed in her old leather smock, and proceeded to work and teach. She had already taught two of The Last Resort mothers to be midwives, and Andy Peyote himself knew all about labor and heating the instruments and cutting the cord. He had seen several births and had also helped carry a dead man from one of The Last Resort domes down the hill to a car. We hear they are teaching death in high school now, another one of those natural functions for which direct experience has given way to a classroom notion.

How does the world look to a child? From an early age, we prepare our children for a world of experts by dividing up their lives for the convenience of the specialists who serve them. They were already on their way to being one-man bureaucracies—their skin for the skin specialist, hair for the barber, mind for the teacher, rhythm for the piano lady, legs for the coach, eyes for the optometrist, imagination for the art instructor—the parents being the chauffeurs and traffic controllers between the various agencies. As they are served by these institutions, so are they learning how to look at themselves, divided and scattered in their parts like the boundaries of occupied cities. From the perspective of The Last Resort, our own children sometimes seemed the most dismembered inhabitants on earth, with a total sense of powerlessness reinforced at every waiting room and on every Yellow Page.

How did Andy Peyote look at himself? We couldn't help comparing him to Pete, another twelve-year-old who lived with his mother in New York but visited his father at The Last Resort during the summer months. Pete, you could say, was getting some of the same experience as Andy Peyote, and if you saw the two of them together, you would pick Pete out as the hippie. Andy looked like a straight kid, with blue jeans and clean shirts and short, combed hair, while Pete wore the beads and had developed Mick Jagger's moves and a defiant expression reminiscent of Ben. He was powerful, in a low-level sort of way, when we took Pete and Chauncey to visit the Red Rocker commune—Pete got Chauncey involved in ripping out the pages of a book. The Rockers didn't put up with that kind of behavior and sent him outside.

Pete was not a juvenile delinquent, he was just a slouchy city kid. In a city environment, he would not be noticed—just another teenager going through a necessary stage of listlessness and rebellion that comes with puberty and with nothing much to do. He had the advantages of commune freedom during the summer, in the sense that he was allowed the same latitude as Andy Peyote, but somehow Pete could never find anything interesting to do. The Last Resort people worried about that for a while, a woman named Pat tried to teach him how to weave and how to work on cars, but Pete has a short attention span. He would never return on his own for more instruction in anything.

Even Andy Peyote, who as Pete's peer would not be expected to notice such things, was always chastising Pete for his immature behavior. There was one incident in particular, at a Sunday barbecue they always had at The Last Resort, where the joints were being passed around and Pete took an extra hard puff to make sure people knew he was smoking. Just like Mark had done in the Cosmic Circle commune. Andy Peyote came over and took the joint away from him, telling Pete that he couldn't smoke unless he stopped acting like a "buffoon."

The difference between them came down to their states of mind. The politeness that we had always mistrusted in Andy Peyote we could now see as a kind of independence, really; he wasn't involved enough with us to need to rebel or to show his power. Pete spent most of his waking hours seeking reactions. He did not do things on their own merits. It severely limited Pete's choices and his sense of himself in the world. Andy could do dishes or walk through the woods; Pete would not let himself be caught doing dishes, and his woods were filled with a lot of walls.

It's impossible to tell whether the other commune children, as they mature, will end up like Andy Peyote. Or even how Andy Peyote will end up. But we left The Last Resort with a renewed feeling about the possibilities of communes. Not so much for their individual survival, but for their system of thinking, which could produce a better-behaved, more resourceful, and more independent child than we had seen elsewhere. Andy Peyote might be just one form of commune child, but he could not have been produced in a conventional environment.

We asked Andy Peyote if he would stay at The Last Resort ultimately, and he said it was possible, but he would have to be voted in by the group. He didn't count on it, any more than he had counted on being let into Mickey's dome with the rat Ponderosa. But he wasn't worried about it. His ultimate goal, he said, was to have "an Opel GT and a log cabin."

That's how it was at The Last Resort, people scamming off the land and living on their wits and ingenuity. They could stay all winter in the cold mountains, spending almost nothing, and then take off for a vacation in Bermuda. When Mickey Peyote got short on cash, he would visit a local college and give a lecture on "alternative lifestyles" for five hundred dollars. The rest of them were equally resourceful. For big projects, they could rely on the commune network.

On the question of commune survival, Mickey Peyote merely pulled out a *Newsweek* and showed us the cover. Food riots, he predicted—part of his general scary prophecy for the world. False sense of security. "They'll be up here someday, those people who put us down. Trying to steal our food." But he had confidence in America's waste, and in his own ability to skim a little off the top once in a while, to make up a life as he went along. Andy Peyote was building the same confidence.

6

The Religious Communes

Andy Peyote became a kind of symbol for the best the communes have produced. It was tempting, in fact, to imagine a whole army of these self-reliant children coming out of The Last Resort and the Red Rockers and the Taos Learning Center to fulfill John Kimmey's dream. It could happen, of course. But not because anybody planned it that way. It is hard to talk about commune children in theory, because in theory their parents have no plan for them. You can look at regular American children in terms of whether they are following the map of their parents' expectations. You can look at the children of the kibbutzim and judge them against the intended results of their communal experiment. But the people at the hangout communes in New Mexico and Colorado and California did not verbalize their hopes for the children; they did not prepare for their children's future in the accustomed way. If anything, life in the informal communes denied the future, and what we sensed at the Ranch was true everywhere: things progressed in haphazard fashion and time did not march. Time oozed. The whole sense of the day was like being on a perpetual acid trip.

There was a popular theory that this way of life was too flaccid and too unintentional to last. Everyone had his own definition of lasting, of course, and of how many years must pass before one could begin to take the communes seriously. A visitor to the Ranch was very impressed with the people getting along together, the spirit of unity, and how all the work got done without any apparent boss, but he ended up denying all that because "this place won't prove itself until after two hundred years." Most of the commune people had a much more modest sense of permanence—Mickey Peyote said that "a permanent commune is one that lasts more than two years." The odds against any of them lasting longer than that, against overcoming all the squabbles and personality conflicts that come from living in close quarters with other people, are very high. The skeptics of the movement say that the only communes with a chance of surviving through several generations are the ones organized around religion. Historically, they say, the only long-lasting communes have been places like certain settlements of the Quakers and the Mennonites, and the Oneida Community.

Some of the old-line spiritual communities still exist in America, but we decided to bypass them in favor of the newer counterculture varieties. There are lots of them around; every movement and nuance of a movement has its religious retreat—Yogis, Sufis, Meher Babans, Gurdjieffians—but the most obvious choice seemed to be the Lama Foundation. Lama is without doubt the Vatican for Americans who have abandoned their Christianity in favor of eclectic Eastern faiths. It is famous as the spiritual home town of Baba Ram Das, who used to be Richard Alpert before he trekked through India and wrote a book called *Be Here Now,* a collection of ramblings about shedding the Western culture and becoming at one with the universe. The Lama Foundation lives off *Be Here Now* as Christianity would live if it derived its entire revenue from royalties on the Bible. Since Ram Das's book sold over one hundred thousand copies, Lama is a very wealthy commune. Its reputation also derives from Ram Das's presence; although the guru doesn't actually reside there anymore, his spirit has left its afterglow, like the track of a radioactive isotope.

Lama is a complex of truly breathtaking adobe buildings set on the highest mountain above Taos. It is invested with that sense of perpetuity that is lacking in the rural communes. The buildings are most impressive—on the scale of the pyramids or Angkor Wat or the Mayan ruins, all built in periods of history when labor was cheap and belief was high. Lama exudes permanence, from its sixty-foot-high central temple with a twenty-foot-wide circular window facing the sun, right down to its outhouses. In most communes you dig deep enough for a couple of years and worry about the future when the shit hits the top. But at Lama, you couldn't see to the bottom of those elaborate A-frame bathrooms that were dug every few hundred yards into the sides of the mountain. The children of Lama couldn't help but believe in the future of this place, with all its majesty and its Byzantine adobe architecture.

Where were the children of Lama? We imagined them to be little grasshoppers, as alien to Chauncey and Bernsie as any children we would run across. We even worried about it, driving up the Lama road, about spiritual deficiency and how the only religion Chauncey and Berns ever got was in discussions of whether or not they were Jewish. But the first thing to notice was the absence of children. The adults were there, all in kaftans and robes, clustered around in small groups, sitting on the grass and chanting to the setting sun. Susan recognized a couple of them, a man named Nizami and Bag Wan Das, a striking six-foot-five hulk of a man with long blond hair to his waist, gauze robes to his ankles, and Marine combat boots on his feet. Bag Wan Das, a former Laguna Beach surfer who became Ram Das's sidekick in India, and Nizami, the nominal head man at Lama, had both met Susan in front of her Nassau beach house, but the recognition did not carry much warmth. It was rather like a meeting between two reformed convicts and a former carouser from the old days—and Nizami and Bag Wan Das were caught between the unpleasantness of a snub and the unpleasantness of an acceptance of their past. They leaned in the direction of the snub. All of the dozen or so people on the grass, actually, nodded with the perfunctoriness of a passing monk whose mind is occupied in higher thoughts. Nizami and Bag Wan Das showed us a tent site —in the woods a good distance down the mountain and completely out of view of the rest of Lama.

The children appeared the following morning in the blue-tiled bathroom inside the central building. Six of them, brushing their teeth. They most definitely didn't look like they belonged to the people on the night shift. For one thing, they were wearing blue jeans and sneakers, or in the case of the girls, simple summer dresses. For another thing, they were cheerful and immediately friendly. We talked to Jerome (eleven) and his sister Carole (nine) about what they did here during the day, and Jerome said, "Nothing much." It was difficult to believe that children of the most prestigious spiritual community in America would have a lot of extra playtime on their hands. But we stood around with the six of them—Jerome and Carole and their younger brother Lee (three), plus Apple (six) and two Oriental girls named Ida and Shoni—and after an hour or so it became obvious that they weren't going anywhere. They were dying for something to do. We asked if we could take them anywhere and Jerome said, "The movies. *Chitty Chitty Bang Bang* is playing in Taos." Not knowing how that bit of secular information got up here, we agreed to take them. It seemed a little risky; I couldn't imagine that their parents would want them subjected to a Disney fantasy, but the six of them pushed the idea and it seemed like a chance to get to know them.

Their parents actually weren't visible around the place during this hour, but right away Jerome said he had to ask his father's permission to go to the movies. It was a strange echo, and totally disorienting: here in a place that called itself a commune, and yet Jerome was worrying about parental permission for a short trek into town. It was only a few miles from Lama that we had first met Andy Peyote, a contemporary of Jerome, running around the countryside.

But all of them said it was necessary, necessary to wait until the grownups were done with their morning prayer meeting before we could go. All of us waited outside a two-foot opening in a gigantic adobe wall for about an hour. You could hear, coming from the room, a progression of Japanese chants, which sounded something like *whoong, hoong, kreech, wach, tchee, joong,* interspersed with *clunks* from woodblocks and *chings* from finger cymbals. A man's voice kept stopping the chants, complaining that they weren't saying the words right. Jerome said Nizami led the group, but Jerome didn't know much about the prayers, where they came from or what they meant. Lama children were not encouraged to attend prayer meetings, which took up three hours of each day and were the basis of the grownups' religious existence.

The door finally opened and all the people who had been on the lawn the night before crawled out—Nizami; Bag Wan Das; his wife, Bavani; a wispy-looking woman with white hair named Layla, who was Apple's mother; a bewildered Ichabod Crane figure called Peer, who was the father of Jerome, Carole, and Lee. Jerome asked about the movies, and Peer said yes without hesitation; none of the grownups were at all concerned about our influence on their children, while by the placement of our tent we knew that they were concerned about our effect on their own spiritual communion.

So we took their children to the movies, and we took them fishing, and we took them everywhere during the ten days we lived at Lama. And we hardly ever saw a grownup, except at dinner, which was a very ritualistic affair when nobody was allowed to talk. Since we were with the children most of the time and we never saw grownups, we deduced that the children never saw the grownups. Jerome and Carole said it was true; they saw their father Peer quite a bit when they stayed in California (about half the year), but when they came on retreat to Lama, they saw him mostly at dinner. The lights at Lama went out right after dinner; the people went directly to sleep in their A-frames scattered through the mountains.

The distance between adults and children here made one aware of how special the camaraderie had been at the other communes. It must have grown on us, in some subtle way, because if we had come to Lama directly from Miami we would not have noticed the children's isolation from grownups. In fact, the situation of Lama children seemed analogous to that of regular children whose parents leave the house every day to go to work. Yet after being with Andy and Mickey Peyote, and the children and grownups at the Ranch and the Taos Learning Center, the Lama children seemed to be deprived. I wondered if we would think the same thing on returning to the world of the nuclear family.

Actually, the children resented their position here. Maybe we encouraged their gripes, but they certainly had a lot of them. Ida was always complaining that she wanted to learn to cook, but that a woman named Zuleikha kicked her out of the kitchen, where food preparation was a religious ritual. Carole complained that she wanted to go to the free school in Taos, but that the grownups wouldn't always drive her down the mountain to meet the bus. There was a lot of grumbling, and other commune children had not complained about their predicaments in quite the same way. These children seemed reduced to the subordinate position of the dissatisfied.

There were things the Lama children might have done, but they never thought of them. A new spiritual center was being built by a group of young teenage believers who had made the trek to Lama from all over the country. True, the workers were somewhat isolated from the pray-ers, and had to live in tents outside the main acreage of the commune, but the children of the insiders were quite aware of the construction project. Jerome, Carole, Ida, and Shoni, who would all have been working at The Last Resort, were not required to participate here. They would not have been prohibited, exactly, but they could not even imagine their own participation. They were listless, listless as Pete had been, without the remotest inkling of their own power. They depended on people like us to create the action. And the only time they did anything together with their own parents was on the special occasions, such as the visit of a famous pantomimist to Lama, when activities were carefully structured and proscribed.

On a religious level, which is what Lama is all about, the children lacked even elementary understanding. Surrounded by their own parents, who called themselves Sufis, the children were not sure what a Sufi was. (Apple said she thought it was people who used false names.) All the children, in fact, had been given new religious names, but they never used them. None of them had read *Be Here Now,* or had it explained to them. We gave them an informal recognition quiz; they all had heard of the Cookie Monster and Yogi Bear, but they weren't sure what yoga was, or who the Dalai Lama was, or what Zen Buddhism consisted of.

All this, of course, is information, and not ultimately important. But even the content of this new religion seemed to pass over them. The message of *Be Here Now* has to do with a kind of mystical thinking that rejects the American fanciful notions of progress and change and things being better in the future. The presentness that we had sensed throughout the less spiritual communes was lacking here. Yet here at the center of the religion Jerome is talking about college and what he wants to be when he grows up. He constantly refers to his father Peer as an "engineer." "But isn't he a Sufi?" "Yeah, but he designs good cars."

So much for the future of Lama. It had the higher purpose, the organization, the deep outhouses, the money, the sense of permanence, yet it did not care about its own children. It cared about other children, and even discussed the idea of taking over the Taos free school as a way to begin to spread its spiritual message. But on a day-to-day level, elements of the religion were absent. It was a paradox. We had come here expecting a pinnacle, a glorious congealing of what we had sensed as the new values of the sloppier communes. And yet we rediscovered the traditional suburban attitudes that the other communes had long since abandoned. Perhaps it had to do with the Lama families traveling back and forth from professional lives to the spiritual retreat, which all of them did. But whatever the reason, Miami came back to us here—in Apple's thumb-sucking (we had not seen a thumb-sucker for several months), in Lee's whining (only Bernsie could outdo him), in Carole and Ida and their complaining, in Jerome and his dependence on tour directors to get him through the day. Other commune people had aired their problems in the open, but here were secrets and whispers. Lee, for instance, was not supposed to know that his mother was coming to visit Lama; it was all part of a messy divorce between Peer and his wife that had not yet been resolved. Peer acted the part of the typically confused father who let his son get away with outrageous temper tantrums. Not a surprising situation for a man who is left with the children—but in other communes, other adults had helped the man work through the problem. I don't think anybody talked to Peer about it.

Nizami, the nominal head of Lama, confirmed what we had observed, at least on a religious level. He said the isolation of the children was deliberate, because children don't know how to pray. "We tried it in the beginning," he said, "but they can't sit still and they interrupt the vibrations and they make it impossible to get high." The complaint is the same one that is making adults move into adults-only condominiums all over the country.

Lama provided at least one hint of why we found very few children in our review of the newer religious sects in America. At the looser communes, children abounded, but at the places with the conscious higher purpose, children are the general nuisance and bother that they have become in many American homes.

There are a few religious movements that take their children more seriously, and one of them is the Hare Krishnas. They are the people you find in every major city in America, dressed in saffron pajamas and sporting shaved heads, dancing and chanting "Hare Krishna, Hare Rama, Hare Rama, Hare Krishna." The Krishna movement started in America in 1968 as a Hindu offshoot but actually has no direct counterpart in India. This perpetual chanting has caught on in America, though, to an incredible extent, and the Krishnas made enough money selling books and incense to consider buying up West Virginia as a separate Krishna nation. The coal miners probably don't have to fear a takeover by the incense empire, but there are several huge compounds of Krishna devotees in America in what turns out to be a well-financed and well-structured religious movement.

We first visited the Hare Krishnas in their Miami compound, where a few teenage men and women were wrapped up in their chants. They didn't stop chanting to question our presence, so Susan and Bernsie could walk right over to the swing where a little girl was sitting alone. She said her name was Laurie and put up four fingers to show her age, and gave a big smile that indicated her missing two front teeth.

The property covered an acre or so, filled with palm trees and an old stucco house with several wooden shacks around it. Laurie led us to one of the shacks, full of holes and termite dribble, which is where Laurie lived. There was a stove in the corner and no furniture except a large discolored foam mattress with two sleeping bags and two blankets on top. In a wistful way, Laurie said that she had no toys, not even a doll. She played with a stuffed monkey, but she said it wasn't really hers.

Bernsie has the instinctive ability to pick out and grab the flashiest object in any room, and the only thing that caught her attention in Laurie's house was a little altar with Indian cloth draped over it and some glass beads piled on top. Berns started to touch it, and Laurie said, "No. You can't do that. It's for Krishna. My mommy made it." Perhaps because she didn't want to seem ungenerous, Laurie offered to let Bernsie see her "deities." She took a little box from the back of the altar, brought it over to Bernsie, and opened it slowly and carefully, as if it might contain a live frog. But there was no frog inside, and not even a deity, just a package of Kleenex and a red pincushion. Laurie looked surprised and disappointed. "The deities must have sneaked away," she said.

Laurie's mother came rushing into the house as if she had gotten word that strangers were alone with her daughter. "Hare Krishna." It was funny to hear it said by somebody so out of breath. "Who are you?" Her name was Bhaktirisa—twenty-one years old, skinny and pale and still in the acne stage.

Susan mentioned Laurie's missing teeth, and how curious it was that they had come out so early. Bhaktirisa told us what happened: "When Laurie was little, she didn't like milk. She cried about it a lot, and I decided to try some other things. So I put Kool-Aid in her bottle, and she would lay there all day with the nipple between her teeth. It made her happy, but after a while, I guess the Kool-Aid just rotted them out.

"But that was before Krishna consciousness," Bhaktirisa said, "and I was very young then. Eighteen. I still didn't know what I was up to." She said that she was three months pregnant now, and very excited about having a child that was "conceived in Krishna."

Susan looked over at the large mattress on the floor and asked Bhaktirisa if it was hard to make love in the bed when her daughter slept right next to her. "Oh, we don't believe in intercourse," she said. "Except to have children. It takes two pints of blood to make semen for one man's orgasm, and it affects him so he can't give all his energy to Krishna." She admitted to "lapses" with her husband, but said having her daughter right there helped remind her. "When I hug my husband, Laurie catches me and tells me, 'Stop. You know you aren't supposed to do that.'" She gave Laurie a pat on the head.

"Why not?" Bernsie asked.

"Because Krishna doesn't like it," Laurie said.

There were no visible children besides Laurie and a few infants, and we asked Bhaktirisa about it. She said that because of all the time spent in chanting and praying and preparing the food, there was hardly any time left for raising children. "Well then, where are they?" Susan asked. Bhaktirisa said all the children in the Krishna movement from the age of five are removed from their parents and sent to a school in Dallas, called Guracula, where they can have the full attention of twenty teachers. They stay in Dallas until they are twelve to fifteen years old, depending on how long it takes them to learn Sanskrit and become Brahmin priests. During those seven to ten years away from home, they will see their parents maybe two or three days out of the year.

It was surprising that those pajamaed chanters you see on the streets had enough money and organization to establish a central school, but they did.

Bhaktirisa said she was happy to serve the movement, and that her daughter Laurie was going to Guracula later that year. "You mean that you would give up seeing your daughter for ten years?"

"It hurt me at first," she said, "to think of my daughter not being here with me. But it's not good to be possessive of our children. And we are not here for ourselves, we are here to serve Krishna. Our children are gifts to him."

Laurie told us she would be glad to go to Guracula because she missed her brother, who was already there. Bhaktirisa took Susan aside to tell her that actually the brother had been sent up for adoption during a period when Bhaktirisa and her husband weren't getting along. Apparently, Bhaktirisa wasn't ready to dash Laurie's hopes about meeting her brother at Guracula.

Guracula has taken over what used to be a Catholic school in the middle of Dallas, a big brick building with classrooms on one side and a church on the other. Some of the Krishna people must have gone to Sunday schools in churches like this, or at least they could identify the cross and the altar as religious objects. They had converted the church almost as abruptly and strangely as they had converted themselves, ripping out the cross and the pews and the songbooks and replacing them with sacred trees and bejeweled mannequins, incense burners and Sanskrit objects they had only recently come to recognize, much less glorify. What you expect to happen when invaders take over your culture.

The four of us took off our shoes, as demanded by the sign, put them in a pile by the door, and went inside. Down the hall were two chubby little boys with shaven heads and pink pajamas, adorable replicas of the people who chant on the streets. They looked Chauncey's age. We were about to walk over to them when a lady dressed in regular clothes intercepted us. "You'll have to see Mohananda," she said.

Mohananda, who occupies the old principal's office, is a red-headed boy-man sitting cross-legged in front of the intercom system. There was a deity chain of pictures behind him, from Krishna on down—all imposing religious figures—but for some reason I wanted to ask him if he had gone to Florida State. He smiled a lot at Chauncey and Bernsie and said we could visit the school if we wanted, but warned us against talking to students. "We do not want them to be distracted by the outside world," he said. He also said there would be nothing for Chauncey and Bernsie to do at Guracula, except maybe catch the chicken pox that had already infected almost every child in the school. Susan didn't want Chauncey and Bernsie contaminated by the devotees, so she took them to museums in Dallas for a few days while I hung around Guracula as much as I could.

The Krishna children were all in classes with the doors closed for most of the morning. Mohananda said they were learning Sanskrit and math. It is not an accredited school, he said, because to be certified in Texas they would have to teach the Alamo along with the Sanskrit, which to him was an unpalatable combination. He was not interested in accreditation anyway, and spoke with open contempt for public schools, calling them "slaughterhouses for children." The twenty-five children now enrolled in Guracula, he said, were kept as isolated as possible from the streets, the parks, and any other places they might run into regular Texas children. There was a big sign on the bulletin board warning young devotees not to associate with other kids in the neighborhood.

At about noon, the doors opened and about twenty children, from the ages of five to ten, all wearing the chiffon costumes, left their various classrooms and headed for lunch. There was a little bit of giggling and jostling, and I approached a group of three boys to ask them if they liked the food around here, but they simply didn't answer. One of the Sanskrit teachers was bearing down on us from behind; he stopped to nudge a boy who was leaning against the wall, apparently trying to get some rest. "You must not tire in the devotion of Krishna," he said, and shoved the boy in the direction of the lunchroom.

The Krishna children eat their meals, which they call "taking *prasadam,*" while sitting cross-legged on a bare linoleum floor with a piece of wax paper for a plate and their fingers for a fork. The boys and girls are segregated into separate dining rooms, just as they sleep in separate dormitories, in accordance with the Hare Krishna belief that men are superior to women. I sat with the boys, who were carefully arranged in a row that followed the contour of the wall around the room. The teachers positioned themselves in the middle of the room and kept an eye on the boys. Something about the scene was reminiscent of a boarding school with all the chairs and tables taken away, but the rigid straight-back postures and the monitored military discipline were still there.

These children seemed so young for boarding schools; a few of them looked to be nine or ten but most of them were no older than Chauncey. One of the smallest boys, who was wearing a cardigan sweater over his Krishna outfit, kept coming over to the teacher and trying to sit on his lap. The teacher, with dispassionate authority, patted the boy on the head and sent him back to his place. Then the boy returned and said he wanted to go to the bathroom. "You know where the bathroom is," the teacher said, and he pointed to the door. Finally, with all his excuses taken away, the boy broke down and started to cry. He said he wanted his mommy, and with the mention of that word "mommy" he was immediately led out of the room by the teacher. Later, the teacher explained that it was only the boy's third day here and his mother was still in town, which aggravated his adjustment problem. "We'll pay a little extra attention to him until he gets over it."

The other boys didn't have much time to react to this scene, because another teacher jumped in front of them and began reciting the blessing. The boys were repeating after him. I only caught part of it, they were talking so fast: "The tongue is the most voracious of the senses, food is false matter." It was the reverse of thanking God for the bounty; the Krishna children were apologizing to God for having to eat the food. A little unsettling for someone who grew up believing that it is responsible, and somehow more reverent, to have that second helping.

The prayer was over, and two adult devotees passed through and put food on our napkins—chick-peas, for the first course; a peppery vegetarian enchilada for the second; a few orange sections for dessert. The drink, ladled into paper cups from a big metal pot, tasted like Kool-Aid cut with tabasco sauce.

After lunch, the room was emptied of children and a hulking character was sweeping the orange peels off the floor. He was Bhaktibob, nineteen years old and working his way into higher consciousness. I asked him about the prayer, and he said that in Krishna life you must deprive yourself of more and more "false sensual matter" until you can live without sex, sleeping, or eating. "Then you would be dead," I said. "No," he corrected me, "then you would be in a blissful state." He said he was down to five hours a night of sleep and one meal a day, which left him more time for chanting and devotion. "The children will go far beyond us," he said. "Already they get up at three-thirty, they spend the day in sweet nectar, chanting and learning the truth of Lord Krishna. They won't have twenty years of false life to get over like I do." Bhaktibob said his father had wanted him to be a football player, because of his size, but he had never liked hitting people. He floundered around in schools before he found Krishna. He asked if I would accept the absolute truth. "It's like an insurance policy," he said. "I never know the moment when I will die, and I want to live in the truth at all times."

The children were on their free period, mostly outside in the yard. But even during the free period there was a certain fear in the air, a lot of glances back over shoulders. The discipline was tight and there was always a teacher lurking around, no trees to climb and no hiding places, no chance to see the children alone. I finally approached a boy in glasses who looked to be the oldest; he was sweeping off a stoop. "Do you have any fun here?" I said.

"Fun," he answered in a slightly cynical tone, "oh yes. We jump around in *artique* [*arati,* the prayer meeting] every day."

"Anything else?"

"Well," he said, "this *is* a free period."

"Yeah," said another boy standing nearby, "free to clean up."

Both these boys knew, to the exact day, how many days they

had lived at the Guracula School. For one of them, it was 362, and for the other it was 243. Both of them had mothers living in the Los Angeles compound, and they both told me the date they had been "brought here." It reminded me of the scratch marks you see on the walls of prisons.

These two boys never said their names, and they were very careful not to come right out and say they didn't like Guracula. But something about the way they talked, a gesture or a movement, made it apparent that they weren't buying this place. We didn't have too long together, just a few phrases back and forth, and then a teacher came over and told me I wasn't allowed to talk to the students. "And if you can't talk about Krishna," he said to them, "then there is no point in talking."

There is a problem as to when you can accept the Krishna consciousness. The Guracula School was aware of it; they had experimented with a few of these eight- and nine-year-olds, kids who had already seen a lot of television and gotten allowances. These few older children were being phased out of the school; their resistance to "submission" was too strong, there was too much goofing off, too much talk about the old world. The older kids were more brazen about talking to me, and their classes, from what I could observe through the windows, were rowdier. I was told by a teacher that they repeatedly got into trouble for trading off their deities, which are kept by each person in a little box under the desk, as if they were baseball cards. They also competed for who had the nicest *dhoti* (the chiffon pants) and who had the best white mark on his forehead. Such games were disturbing to the leaders, and they had brought in an ex-Marine to teach the advanced Sanskrit class and restore the reverence.

The ideal age for a potential devotee, Mohananda told me, was five years old, and the school had cut off further admissions to any older children. About fifteen of their students were five-year-olds; these children were put in separate classes and slept in a separate dormitory so they wouldn't be contaminated by the eight-year-olds.

I could sense the difference between these two groups of children even in their response to me. The older ones were trying to

141

tell me something; the younger ones acted as if I were from another planet. Around the primary school, the younger children were learning the names of Hindu deities through the use of Montessori flash cards. One of the boys, Bhaktibret, had a habit of standing right in front of me and staring with a puzzled look on his face. After one of the classes, when we all walked to the showers, he finally got up the courage to ask me some questions. He wanted to know about Jack and the Beanstalk. "Is it true," he asked, "that a man can climb to the sky on a big plant, and meet giants there?" Rag-nav, the primary teacher, overheard our conversation and rushed over to explain that it was an earlier teacher who told the class about Jack; Rag-nav didn't want me to think he was responsible. "We don't teach them those fantasies anymore," he said. "They don't need fantasies, except for playing father and mother to prepare them for marriage." Rag-nav asked Bhaktibret to tell me a real story about Krishna. And he did. It was about a crow who bragged that he was faster than Krishna. And how Krishna turned himself into an arrow and followed the crow in the air until the crow was exhausted and fell to the ground, fully expecting to be pierced by the arrow. But the arrow landed right beside him instead. And the crow submitted to Krishna.

Bhaktibret, waddling along on chubby legs, kept trying to place me. "You are a devotee, aren't you?"

"No."

He looked disappointed, and asked what I ate. I told him meat and he looked more disappointed.

"Do you eat lollipops?" he asked.

"Sometimes. Do you?"

"No . . . Do you take prasadam?"

"Sometimes," I said, even though today was the first time.

He thought for a minute and then gave me a broad smile like he had solved the problem. "Then you are half *karmee* [heathen] and half devotee." He was delighted to find a way to include me in his Krishna world.

I asked about his mother, and he said, "My karmee mother, or my spiritual mother?" None of the older kids had made that distinction. It turned out that the two mothers he was talking about were actually one and the same lady. Bhaktibret had learned to divide his mother into entirely different people, the one who existed before Krishna consciousness and the one who found Krishna.

He was fascinated by my tie-dyed shirt, and asked me to make one for him. "I didn't make it," I said, "I bought it." He looked confused. "Why didn't you make it?"

"Because I don't know how."

"Well, then why didn't you tell your wife to make it?"

Walking with these kids through the Hare Krishna corridors, it felt like a Charles Dickens fantasy. I couldn't get over the spareness and cruelty of the place, the straw mats on the floor where the children slept in the room together; the boy who still had chicken pox, lying with his head on the linoleum and orange peels scattered about him like the garbage around a zoo animal; the way the teacher made the sick boy get up and come to class because "his spirit will get sick from missing the lessons, and a spiritual sickness is greater than a physical one."

It was cruel and repressive, the way Rag-nav made them take cold showers and wouldn't let them horse around in the communal shower stall—they could see bodies but not touch them, they referred to their parts as "anus" and "genitals" and their shit as "stool"; no mirth in witnessing their body functions. They hardly laughed at all, which was unusual for a group of five-year-olds, and they looked constantly tired.

It is hard to take a religion seriously when the teachers and priests are all nineteen-year-olds who can't quite hide their own confusion about things. Rag-nav the teacher was somebody I got past the absolute truth with; he wanted to provide the little children with a progressive education and a lot of plastic learning toys that he called "attachments." But there weren't many attachments in the classroom, and he was forced by his superiors into a lot of spanking and knuckle-rapping that made him uncomfortable.

I asked where he came from to be teaching all these children, and he said a middle-class family.

"Well, did you get along with your parents?"

"No, I resented them, because they never stopped to wonder where my head was at."

"Do you wonder where these kids' heads are at? What if there is a child here who could make a good doctor or lawyer or has a curiosity about machines or butterflies. What chance does he have to find out for himself?"

"We don't want lawyers. We want philosophers. This school is to produce the priests of tomorrow."

"Can a philosopher be produced?"

"With love," Rag-nav said. "Love is the difference. I'm trying to teach these children something, something I care about."

"But do they have a choice? They are forced to chant Krishna."

"We have discipline, it is true. But it is discipline given with love."

Rag-nav directed the kids in the afternoon artique, which is where they learn to respect the deities and do the Krishna cere-monial dance. There are fifteen little kids in this line, facing an altar of little dolls they have made, and this grownup hovering behind them: "Shape up, this isn't Grand Central Station, Hare Krishna, Hare Krishna, give back that deity, Bhaktigeorge, it's not yours, Hare Krishna, Hare Rama, Bhaktibret, it's not blissful to kick Bhaktijean." It could have been the pledge of allegiance they were saying, for all the effect it had on them. Krishna con-sciousness was a pervasive daily occupation, but it sure didn't stop unruly behavior.

This children's artique was a warm-up for the regular worship, which takes place every day at 3 A.M. I got up from a motel and ate a candy bar and drove into town. A man dressed in white robes, who I hadn't seen before, opened the door and said how auspicious was my coming. He said the artique would begin in a few minutes and handed me the *Bhagavadgita* to read while I waited. I pretended to read, but my eye was out for the children. They started showing up about 2:45 A.M., some yawning, some with sleep still in their eyes. They had the droop of raw recruits on their first morning of boot camp. The boy with glasses had to sweep all the floors, because, he said, he had laughed during the Sanskrit lesson.

All of them, children and grownups, congregated in the center of the church, a gigantic glistening hall made larger by the fact that the pews are gone. In front, where the cross used to be, is an icon of a black female saint, dressed in jewels and wreathed in incense. Everybody stands around in the drowsiness of 2 A.M. pinball players until Mohananda starts to play the harmonium set up on the floor. The people begin to sway and chant. Then they start throwing their hands into the air and chanting louder and walking around in an ever-widening circle. After fifteen minutes, the walk turns into a run, a stampede of circling worshipers, and I find myself right in the path of forty charging Hare Krishnas. There is nothing to do but hold up my hands and run as fast as everybody else out of self-defense. At 3 A.M. the adults are rushing around a cold floor with bare feet, repeating Hare Krishna an uncountable number of times. The children stumble along and try to keep up as best they can.

The Krishna children were certainly not ignored like the Lama children had been (although in fact their isolation in Dallas was part of a similar desire on the part of the parents—to put devotion ahead of kinship). I couldn't help feeling that the Lama children, being left alone, were better off. The Krishna children struck me as prisoners. It could have been the mere result of my rejection of their religion, for a child can always be called a prisoner of his parents' culture. If we had met these children, or children like them, in India following the same daily routine, perhaps we would not have been horrified. In Texas, we were profoundly horrified.

We had a similar reaction to the Jesus freaks. We visited several Jesus-freak communes across the country, places that had the look of the rural hangout communes except they were usually shabbier and less well kept up. Jesus-freak parents were about the same age as Hare Krishna parents, people in their early twenties with babies or very young children. In fact, while Jesus freaks and Hare Krishnas think of each other as archideological enemies, they seem alike in almost every respect—certainly in their treatment of children. Substitute the Bible for the *Bhagavadgita* and Jesus for the black icon, and the story of Guracula is the story of the Jesus communes—rigid discipline, prodigious use of the apple switch, long hours of praying and chanting, isolation from the rest of the world. And yet somehow, there is a noncompliance on the part of the children. That was part of the feeling of a prison in these places; you always got the idea that somehow the children weren't buying it. For all the beatings (and we stayed at one Jesus commune where children were routinely beaten several times a day), the children were not as well behaved as The Last Resort children had been.

None of these religious communities really captivated our attention. Something would ultimately happen to all these little Guracula children and Jesus children, but what was happening now did not interest us as much as life in the hangout communes. We saw nothing in the religious raising of children that could challenge our own notions. They were throwback cultures, really, throwbacks to a time of "spare the rod and spoil the child," and of living out words in the holy books. In contrast to the unorganized spirituality in the Taos valley, a spirituality of people working together, the spirituality here was formulistic and ultimately impersonal. It didn't matter who the children were, really, as long as they learned to follow the routine. In that sense, the Jesus freaks and Hare Krishnas failed to reach their own children.

7

Synanon

None of the preceding communes had tried to affect its children's behavior in a systematic way. The urban places were involved in psychology, but they were too close to conventional America to be very unique. The rural hangout places were creating something unique, but it was all done informally and chaotically. The religious communes had the organization that the rural communes lacked; but they either ignored the children or else they tried to fit the children into a formulistic mold. There were only two places that combined the rigorous structure of the religious communes with a programmed attempt to uplevel the children's behavior. Two places that, on the surface, seemed diametrically opposed to one another. One was Synanon, the modernistic drug-rehabilitation community with overtones of 1984; and the other was the Farm, the biggest and most influential of the hippie communes.

After months of traveling through rural communities where people were trying to recapture the simplicity of America's past, it was a science-fiction-like jolt to arrive at Synanon, a well-run chain of communities along the coast of California. Synanon is basically a large corporation whose business is the reclamation and reformation of drug addicts, and its success is advertised in the fact that not only do the ex-addicts live in the community, but living side by side with them are self-imposed exiles of the middle class. It is strange to think of these two groups living together, because usually they are considered natural enemies.

What made the addicts come to Synanon is easy enough to discover. In 1958, Chuck Dederich, himself an ex-alcoholic, set up a halfway house in Santa Monica as a place where addicts of one sort or another could be helped to kick their habit. Dederich's plans to rehabilitate these victims of society through cold-turkey cures and group therapy did not turn out the way he had hoped. Those who successfully kicked their habit after several months at Synanon returned to the outside world as Synanon graduates ready to try again for a normal life. Too often they failed and began drinking or taking drugs again, and many of them returned to Synanon for some postgraduate work. Eventually, Dederich saw that no matter how far the addicts went toward rehabilitation at Synanon, they failed in the outside world. It is not uncommon for social workers, prison reformers, and the like to complain about society and to blame its structure as the cause of all the crime and misery that takes place. What is uncommon is for them to take their complaints seriously, and try to devise alternatives. This is what Chuck Dederich did. Soon there were no more Synanon graduates; those who left were called "splittees." The outside world was seen as an unreformable ugly place. They began to call it "the street."

If it was the reality of "the street" which brought the drug users to Synanon, then it was the "specter of the street" which brought the middle-class families there. These non-drug-using voluntary members of Synanon are called "lifestylers," and they choose to live at Synanon because over the years Synanon has developed a strict code of behavior and philosophy. The basic rules are: "no drugs, no alcohol, no tobacco, and no physical violence or any threat of physical violence." Synanon's philosophy contains goals like "to love and be loved, to learn, to be safe and healthy." This was very reassuring to those who found that suburbia wasn't as safe as they had hoped it would be. The middle-class fathers and mothers didn't want to have to worry about pushers lurking at the public high school, about their daughter being raped or kidnapped, about their ten-year-old son being hit on his way to school by a drunk driver. Nor did they want to cope with the general problems of sex education, rebellious children, birth-control pills, disinterested teachers, and the isolation which comes from being a suburban nuclear family.

Though they were no longer individually wealthy (in order to live at Synanon the lifestylers had to give all their money to the community), collectively they were wealthy and safe, and could always answer the question "Do you know where your children are tonight?" Even if their children were five hundred miles away, they had gotten there on the Synanon jitney, and were staying at another Synanon community.

Synanon now has about sixteen hundred people living in its various centers, and there are over two hundred sixty children under the age of eighteen. Some of these children have lived their whole lives at Synanon as children of former addicts or life-stylers.

Synanon's major concern is the rehabilitation of people with personality disorders, a very marketable product, and that is how Synanon supports all the people who live here. People and corporations who have an interest in reforming drug addicts donate goods, services, and money to the tax-exempt Synanon Foundation. The addicts themselves have a business, selling personalized office supplies, and the lifestylers either maintain their outside jobs and put the money they make into Synanon, or they work directly for Synanon.

We drove up to Tomales Bay, one of the Synanon properties north of San Francisco, and were met at the gate by a plump girl wearing a lot of green eye makeup, jangly earrings, high-heeled shoes, and a dress that *Cosmo* might have recommended for the working girl several years ago. She introduced herself as Lynn, and said that she had made arrangements for us to visit the nursery where the children lived when they were between six months and two years old. We were a little early for our 11 A.M.

appointment and she suggested that we take a walk. "The nursery isn't a place where you can drop in any old time, it's quite a wonderful place for the children, their very own environment, and it's very well run," she said. "They don't like a stream of visitors constantly interrupting the children's day and whether you're a parent or a visiting sociologist you've got to call up first."

We didn't realize that the children did not live with their parents, and Lynn explained the Synanon system to us. Women in their late pregnancy left their Synanon jobs and moved to the Hatchery, part of the Oakland complex. Here, the women learned about childbirth and infant care, and here they lived with their babies from the time they were born till they were six months old. The women shared baby-sitting chores, even nursing each other's children, and were generally good support for one another during the period of postnatal depression.

The nursery was a small red house surrounded by a tidy yard filled with large rubber balls and sturdy climbing frames. Around the yard was a locked chain-link fence. Lynn buzzed, and out came another contact, named Elaine, who took us toward the house. Chauncey and Berns went off to climb on the frames, but Elaine told them to get off, the frames were just meant for the little kids. They got off and began a game with the balls, and again Elaine told them the balls were for the little kids, and that they had to be immediately available when the little kids wanted them. We told Chauncey and Berns to sit on the porch.

Elaine showed us the "large muscle workshop." It contained carpeted ramps and steps, bridges and big cushions. One entire wall was covered by a mirror; the whole room was a Vic Tanney's for toddlers. A few children were crawling through a wooden tunnel. The room was spotless and uncluttered. "The room you see here," Elaine said, "is to encourage the children's large muscle motor control. This room, along with the others you will see, are completely safe for the children who live here. Now, we have eight of them; they go from eight months up to two years old. We believe that a child must have a safe environment in which to grow. And do you know, one of the most danger-producing factors we have here is our visitors. They come in and leave the door open, or track dirt or glass in on their shoes, or maybe someone leaves an open pocketbook on a low table. We give the house a constant checkup to avoid such dangers." Some literature Elaine had given us about bringing up babies at Synanon included the sentence, "Our children's environment will be safe if we *constantly* assume that it is not."

The next room was the "small muscle workshop." It looked like a display case for creative playthings. Groups of wooden educational toys were displayed on low tables. The floor was thickly carpeted, and over the carpet was a plastic mat and large pillows. A pile of cloth books lay near the pillows. Beyond the small muscle room were the sleeping rooms. The beds were little boxes on the floor, covered with bright quilts and stuffed toys. The walls were brightly painted. Elaine said they didn't want to inhibit the children, so they didn't keep them in traditional cribs and playpens. The area was completely sanitized for the children's wanderings. Elaine called it a *"no*-less environment." No toy was sharp enough to pierce, fragile enough to break, small enough to be swallowed. The doorjambs were padded and the doorknobs placed beyond the children's reach.

Susan asked Elaine if she didn't think Synanon was overprotecting the children. She answered by telling her to lower her voice, because the children didn't like loud sounds. Then she said that the children were not overprotected, but were as free as scientists to explore their world—and that the children often played without adult supervision since there were only two adults in attendance.

Several kids were crawling around the house, some playing on the grass outside, some sitting on the porch. We heard no one cry and saw no fights. In the middle of the changing room, filled with spotless piles of diapers and shelves full of ointments, were some large record books on a counter. One was a record of all visitors; our names were there. The other was a record of each child's day. The notations included details on bowel movements: frequency and color; night behavior: bed-wetting, bad dreams; eating habits; general health; whether or not the child had visitors.

Elaine interrupted our reading to inform us that the files made it easier for the different adult shifts to take over from one another. They didn't have to ask each other about each child; it was all written down. Everything was written down at Synanon, from the most minor instructions to the most elaborate expositions of philosophy. A characteristic statement on children said: "We want to inspire trust . . . that is, their environment is always safe, they are always cared for with love and respect, their food is always properly prepared, their good health is always of prime importance, there are always interesting toys and equipment for them to enjoy. And as our infants live in this dependable world, they can count on being able to relax because there is no fear or lack . . . and learn to know themselves."

This involvement with professionalism was an attitude not found in the other places we visited. For the most part the women in rural communes wanted to be involved with all aspects of their children's lives, believing in their own common sense, and putting down much of the educational and medical mystique. Here mothers not only believed in expertise, but gave up their children to be raised by experts.

"What about the children's mothers?" we asked Elaine. "When do the kids get to see them?"

"That depends on where she works. Chuck Dederich and the board of regents try to get a mother a job near her child, but that isn't always possible. If the mother lives in Oakland or San Francisco she sees her child around once a week. If she lives up around Tomales Bay, she sees him more often. As a matter of fact, one of the aides working here now has a child in the nursery, and she sees him every day. There aren't any rules about it."

The next age group of children lived in the Oakland complex, a block of apartment buildings owned by Synanon. One wing of buildings was devoted to the kindergarten. The cleanliness of the nursery was continued here, but now the children themselves were taking part in the maintenance of their rooms, which were bright and cheery, and in fact very much like the nursery quarters. Their rooms were called caves, and bedrooms were segregated by sex. The demonstrators, as Synanon teachers are called, lived nearby. There were about four beds to a room, each bed the private space of the child who occupied it, covered with the belongings he had taken with him from the nursery. The walls were sprinkled with posters, many of them sayings by Chuck Dederich, such as: "Why remain an idiot any longer than necessary?" "It's better to be rich and healthy rather than sick and poor." "If you win all your Synanon games you lose your life."

The children, involved with putting away their clothes and sweeping the floor, were very friendly, inquisitive, and responsive. When we asked their names, or how old they were, they told us, but gave out a lot of other information as well. They told who their mothers and fathers were, what jobs they had at Synanon, and whether their parents had come to Synanon as drug addicts or lifestylers. (Synanon has a ritual called "playing your tapes," which means giving a rundown of your past history to a stranger. These little kids had no tapes of their own, so they played their parents'.) One little boy, around five, who looked like a clean midget version of Steve McQueen, said, "My mommy and daddy had terrible fights and he beat her up, and was always sticking a needle into his arm, but now we are at Synanon and they don't fight anymore."

When the Synanon children are four they learn how to play the Synanon game, a form of encounter which could actually be considered the Synanon religion. The game started many years before as encounter therapy for drug addicts. It was such a successful way of dealing with problems that the lifestylers also began to play it. There are even Synanon game clubs in cities that do not have Synanon communities. Each game is played by about a dozen people, and those living at Synanon are required to play a certain number of games each month. While we were there a group of four-year-olds had their first lesson. It was after an art class, and their demonstrator told them to clean up, because they were going to do something very special. They cleaned up carefully, washing off all their brushes, then their hands, and finally the sink. The demonstrator had arranged eight chairs in a circle.

"All right, children, today we are going to have our first lesson in how to play the Synanon game. Do any of you know what the game is?"

Some of the children had been at Synanon only a few months, others for several years, but they all knew what the game was and answered with a loud, enthusiastic yes. The demonstrator told them that she was very pleased with them, and then she gave each child a golden loop of ribbon that would easily fit over his head, and she told the children to put the loops on. "Now, when we put these loops around our heads we shall say 'in the game' and when we take them off we all say 'out of the game'! Now let's everybody do it." The children did this with only a slight bit of self-conscious giggling.

The demonstrator went on. "When we have our loops on, and we are in the game, we can say anything we want to, and not get into trouble for it. We can yell and scream and say words we aren't supposed to when we aren't in the game. What we can't ever do is to hit someone. That's very important, children, never to hit someone. Do you all understand that? [She was answered by a chorus of yesses.] Now let's play the game. Put on our loops and say 'in the game.'" They all put their loops on.

For a moment the children hesitated, and then following the lead of one little boy they all began to shout at once. First they just made noise, and then they began shouting adult obscenities and finally they moved along to the words they really knew were dirty, like *shit* and *ca-ca* and *doodoo,* and one kid went so far as to say "Nancy eats doodie." Their demonstrator listened to them for a while and then she told them to take off their loops and say "out of the game." She told them that they all did well in their first game, and asked them if they knew some other things to say in the game besides curse words. Some raised their hands and told her, "You can get mad at somebody," "You can tell somebody something and not get punished," "You can tattle on someone if they did something bad."

"Yes, yes, those are all very good answers, and there are special words to use when you do all those things, and special ways to go about it. But we don't want to do too much today. I can see that you are all going to be very good game players because today you showed me that you know how to use a game opportunity. Tomorrow we will learn how to indict someone. Can you say that word? All right, to indict someone means that you want to tell them about something they did that you don't like. You can indict anyone, someone in your room, or class, your parents, or demonstrators. Here is an example. Let's say that Noelle was using blue paint in art class, and Jill took it away from her and wouldn't give it back. Instead of Noelle getting mad at her and maybe having a fight, she could come and tell me about it, and tell me that she wanted to indict Jill. Then we would call a game about it, and we would all sit around in a circle and try to work it out. Everyone could say something about it, who is right, and who is wrong. That way we can avoid fights and secrets and people ganging up on each other. And if people have their feelings hurt, we will know about it, and try to help them." The kids finished their game lesson and ran out for ice cream.

Synanon had assumed full responsibility for the children, on every level that traditionally belongs to the actual parents. The children's acclimatization to their environment was handled by the demonstrators, and reinforced by other members of Synanon. The children learned the accepted Synanon behavior, and jargon, in their houses, at school, in the dining room—everywhere they were met by the same standards.

Discipline was handled in the game. As one ten-year-old explained it: "If we do something bad, we get indicted, and somebody calls a game on us, and then they game us and game us until we shape up. But they call this a nonviolent place, which means that nobody ever hits us unless something really terrible happens, like somebody burns a building down, or something. And then the demonstrator has to check with the board of regents if it's all right to spank us."

Synanon was also in charge of such things as handing out an allowance, which it did not only to the children at Synanon, but to everyone. It was called walking around money, or W.A.M. The amount was based on how long the recipient had been at Synanon, and the amount never exceeded fifty dollars a month. No one at Synanon ever had to make a decision based on whether or not he had enough money to do something. But the board of regents decided such important things as should a couple get married, or should they have a baby—based on factors like emotional maturity and good health.

All this teaching and decision-making had once been the mother's role, and we wondered how the Synanon mothers felt about their loss of power. Most of the women were very happy with the way Synanon was arranged. They felt that Synanon could give their children things that they as individual mothers never could, both materially and emotionally. They were glad to be able to have a job without feeling guilty about abandoning their kids—and they were also free to spend more time with their husbands or boyfriends. The women thought it was better for the children to see their mothers as role models who did many things, rather than just as "mother." They felt that the children here would not turn into "mother lovers," the Synanon term for someone who is overdependent on his parent.

The children were also very positive about their living arrangement. The older kids who had lived in nuclear families before coming to Synanon remembered fights and family pressures that simply did not exist here. Even though most of the children said they liked being away from their parents, we saw at least one case where this wasn't true, in which a little girl was not happy about the amount of time she spent with her mother. Unlike the outside world, though, where for the most part that kind of a problem remains unspoken and unresolved, at Synanon the children could always call a game. One such game had been called by a twelve-year-old girl who was indicting her mother. The game was held in the corner of the school library after school was out, and it included Dianne, the girl who called the game; her mother, Wendy; two younger sisters; a few schoolmates; and two demonstrators. Dianne spoke first; she was very poised and serious: "I called this game because I want to indict my mother for not spending enough time with us, and for making plans that she doesn't keep."

"Wait a minute," said one of Dianne's sisters. "You called this game, we didn't. I don't have any complaints right now, so don't go saying 'us' when you really mean 'you.'"

"OK. I mean that I'm getting fed up with how my mother makes plans to see me, and then at the last minute she calls to say she's too busy. Or if I do see her, she seems to have something on her mind and she doesn't pay any attention to me at all."

Her mother answered, "Oh, Dianne, it's only happened once or twice. You know I've just started working with the kindergarten and it's been very hectic getting used to it."

"No," said Dianne, her voice getting a little shaky. "It's happened more than that, so don't go blaming your job. We plan on doing something, and then I look forward to it, and it doesn't happen."

Dianne's younger sister said, "Well, I know what she means. Mother does cancel out sometimes. The thing is, Dianne gets much more upset than we do."

"Well, I don't see why you don't get upset. After all, she is our mother!" Dianne said.

A demonstrator intervened: "Wait a minute, Dianne. That statement doesn't mean anything. Why not try dealing with her as a person who has a lot of work to do, and who has to figure out a better way to manage her time instead of trying to solve things by using loaded words like *mother*."

Dianne's mother interrupted. "Well, it's true that a lot of our plans haven't worked out lately. The younger ones don't seem to care, but Dianne makes these demands on me that I just don't seem to be able to handle. I seem to be swamped by her."

Dianne was crying by now, and angry. "I don't see what is so swamping about my wanting to spend time with you. I think you are just a mean old bitch."

Her mother answered, "Dianne, you nag at me all the time for one thing or another, and sometimes I just don't want to see you."

157

One of Dianne's younger sisters said, "It's true about Dianne, she always finds something to pick on."

One of the demonstrators said, "Look, I think that Dianne needs more from Wendy than she can give right now. But Dianne, you have to be realistic and see that Wendy is busy with her job. And Wendy, you can't just ignore the whole thing and hide behind your work, you have to pay attention."

One of the other children in the group suggested, "Why couldn't Dianne and Wendy spend some time together without the other kids? The other kids wouldn't care, and then Dianne and Wendy could talk about things."

The demonstrator said that might be a good idea, and the game went on to someone else. When the game was over Susan talked with Dianne's mother. "You know, when Dianne called you a bitch I was really horrified, it was almost as if I were saying it to my mother. There were many times I certainly wanted to, but there was no way I ever would. She would have killed me."

"The game is set up for that very purpose. That's one of the first things the little children learn, that in the game you can say anything, and it's all right. These kids play the game so much better than I do because they learned it when they were very young. We've been here for five years. They take it very seriously and it comes naturally to them."

"Yes, I understand that, but didn't you mind? I would have minded if someone called me that."

"No, I didn't mind, I didn't take it personally, if you know what I mean. I envy them their openness. They are fearless when it comes to expressing their feelings. They know nothing bad will come of it. It's much harder for me to be honest, after years of keeping things to myself. Sometimes I don't even want to tell the truth, or even face it. I would much rather push it aside, but you can't do that here."

"But what about your powers as a parent, what are they?"

"That concept doesn't really exist around here. We are a community who share the same feelings about things. Sometimes I would like to hide behind the traditional role of the parent saying

'Do what I say because I'm your mother!' But you can't do that here. In being able to live your life as something other than just a parent you also become just a person in the eyes of your children. I'm not the powerful, mysterious mother to my children that my mother was to me. Sometimes I resent not being that mother; the children question everything all the time. For someone like me, it's often hard to take."

Susan knew what she meant, because she found it disconcerting to talk to the Synanon kids. The children were very verbal, not just for commune kids, but any kids. Talking to a bunch of ten-year-olds, you could not hide behind the fact that you were a writer or an adult, and there was really no such thing as an interview. Whatever questions you asked them, they had a bunch ready to ask you back. They wanted to know how we could write a book about kids if we weren't sociologists or someone specially trained for this type of work. They asked if we were married. When they found out Susan was a widow, they wanted to know if she would get married again. These questions would have been considered bad manners in suburbia; but at Synanon, where everyone empties out the pockets of his soul once or twice a week, these personal questions were just small talk as far as the kids were concerned. There were no secrets at Synanon. Besides the personal games that happened spontaneously, there were long open games called stews which any kid could attend. They could hear a teacher being put down because he was on a "superstar ego trip," because he liked to hear himself talk and sometimes forgot that his job was to teach; a fight between two men because one had slept with the other's wife; their parents being told off because they were not doing their jobs well enough.

The ten-year-old girls in Dianne's game had recently moved out of their dorm, a huge airplane-hangar-like building which slept forty kids in the same long room. Now they were living in a small house with eight other kids, boys and girls their own age. They were proud of their new house. It had much the same air about it as did the other houses, with the same Dederich posters on the wall. The house had a large central living room filled with beanbag cushions, desks, and a television. On each side of the living room were two bedrooms and a bathroom, one side for the boys, the other for the girls. From this center, the kids got themselves to school, meals, and jobs without constant adult supervision. When they needed grownup help they got in touch with their "deschooler," who is the person in charge whenever the children are not in their classroom. But they didn't like to contact him much. They took a great deal of pride in the fact that they could care for themselves, as part of the Synanon community. This pride motivated a lot of their behavior, and it's what made possible a trip to the dentist in which only two adults were needed to watch fifty kids. They made the long trip to town in a big bus with the name Synanon written in large letters across each side of the bus. Each child felt it his duty to behave well for Synanon, and while six kids at a time went into the dentist's, the others sat quietly on the lawn.

This belief in Synanon is what made the children want to keep their house clean and orderly. Otherwise they would have to move back to their dorm. This would have meant a great loss of face, and so Dianne, the oldest girl in the house, called a game so the group could work out its problems of living together. Dianne and another girl went to the dining room, which was always open, and made fudge bananas for everyone to eat when the game was over.

The kids—there were around ten of them—trooped into the living room and sat in a circle on the floor. They were all between the ages of nine and twelve. Dianne said, "I called this game because I want everybody to have a nice time in this house, and I want us to all work together, and first of all I'm going to put the game on Amber. Last night you played loud games in the living room and you kept me up till at least twelve o'clock."

Amber: I did no such thing.

Gregg: Yes you did. I heard you. You were jumping on the pillows and giggling and saying "shhh." We can't stay here if you act like that, we'll get sent back to the dorm.

Another kid: Yes, Amber, you are very selfish a lot of the time. You make a mess in the living room, and then you don't clean it up. You expect somebody else to do it.

Cynthia: Yes, Amber, who do you think we are, your maids? Well, maybe somebody else is, but I'm not.

Amber: I clean up as much as anybody, and nobody has to tell me, especially you, miss bossy bitchy Dianne. You think you're something because you're almost thirteen and can lord it over the rest of us and be snobby and all that. Well, I don't think it's fair.

Dianne: Well, somebody has to see that things run smoothly here.

Amber: It certainly doesn't have to be you! And now the game is on Cynthia, with all her little stuffed cats on her bed and her trust fund because her daddy's rich; she is just one fucking spoiled rich kid, talk about being selfish! [Cynthia's father was divorced from her mother and did not live at Synanon.]

Lucy: Well, it's true, Cynthia. You are always talking about having money one day, and what you'll do with it. How do you think that makes us feel? And then your mother's friend comes by here on a motorcycle and gives you a ride and you don't offer one to anybody . . .

Cynthia: It's not my fault if I have money and you don't, and if somebody offers me a ride how can I share these things?

Dianne: No, Cynthia, don't make it sound silly, like you don't know what we're talking about. It's your attitude that people don't like. Now what do you have to say?

Cynthia doesn't say anything, and all the kids try to get her to talk. Tears begin to roll down her cheeks. The deschooler comes in. He sits in the circle and quietly listens to all this, and then he tells Cynthia that she isn't using the game to her advantage, and that in order to learn something she has to say something. But Cynthia remained silent, and the deschooler, whose name was Sam, turned to Lucy and said, "Lucy, what about this problem that Dianne said she was having with you? She said that you follow her everywhere she goes."

Lucy: Well, if you call walking next to someone following them then I guess you could say that. But I never noticed anything like that. I thought Dianne was my friend.

Dianne: I am your friend, Lucy, but that doesn't mean you have to go everywhere I go, and be such a copycat.

Lucy: Well, I'm not a copycat. Just because I happen to be doing the same thing that you are doesn't mean that I am a copycat. I'm not doing it because you're doing it. You don't own all the ideas in the world, do you, you fucking snob? And anyway, you really hurt my feelings the other day when we were walking somewhere and Amber came over and asked if you wanted to go to the dining room with her and you said yes and the two of you went off and left me standing there.

Amber: Yes, Lucy, you don't have to go everywhere. People don't always have to be together, do they?

Cynthia: That's true, Lucy. You really don't have any of your own ideas. And another thing, you're always eating. That's your idea, but it's not a very good idea. But that's not my problem.

Dianne: No, that's her problem, and the boys' . . .

They all laugh at this except Lucy who now has tears rolling down her cheeks. She sort of blubbers when she cries. The demonstrator asks her what's going on.

Lucy: It seems to me that I'm just a great big fucking bore and a drag on everyone and I have no friends.

Amber: No, that's not true, Lucy. We all like you, it's just that you have to give people more room, I guess is the best way to say it.

Cynthia: Well, I want to put the game on George, for hitting me the other night. I don't think it's fair for him to use his strength like that.

George: Oh come on, Cynthia. You're just mad at me because I was roasting marshmallows for some other girls, and not just you.

Cynthia: That's not true.

Lucy: Oh yes it is, because she told me that she was mad at you. You can't use the game like that, Cynthia, it isn't right. You have to indict him for the real reason, otherwise there's no point.

George: Listen, Cynthia, I still like you even if I did do all that, and you can't be such a fucking bitch about everything.

162

And now I want to put the game on Sam. Why won't you let us watch television, you old windbag?

Sam: Because this place is just one big mess. Get it cleaned up, and stop fighting with each other, and you can start watching it in a few days.

None of the kids like this answer and they all start calling him names. He listens for a while and then he tells them he doesn't think they'll have any problem working things out, they've known each other for years and they can pull themselves together. Dianne decided that the game was over at this point, and she and Cynthia went out to get the fudge bananas.

Not only did the children use the game to straighten out problems in their own lives, they also used it to impose a hypothetical morality on the outside world. "If the game were played on the street" was a common notion the children used when they talked about life in America, and what was wrong with it. They also used the idea in their schoolwork; pinned to the various bulletin boards throughout the school I saw papers entitled "If Nixon had played the Synanon game there would have been no Watergate." That there was no game "on the street" was a fact upon which the children could depend to explain why Synanon was so much better off than the street. The children didn't realize just how similar to America Synanon is; it was just that Synanon had its own uses for the conventions and traditions of America.

The oldest girls, who were between the ages of fourteen and seventeen, lived together in a house called the Finishing School. On a typical evening they were all sitting in front of the TV set watching a Sandra Dee movie. Their hair was in rollers, and they were doing their nails and glancing through calorie counters. One girl explained: "Since everyone stopped smoking here two years ago we've had a real problem with being overweight. I guess it's really been worth it, though, to stop smoking. It has given us moral ascendancy." Over who, we wanted to know.

"Well, over those who still smoke, I guess."

"But what difference does it make, if you think you're better than anyone else?" Susan asked.

"We are better in a lot of ways, and it's good not to forget it.

We are rich kids here, and we take French lessons and learn to play tennis, and we have leisure time."

"What do you do in your leisure time?"

"Tomorrow we are going to rearrange the furniture, and then we've called a game with the boys. We want to hang out with them, but a lot of them are rude, and just involved with maintaining a tough image." And there it was; these girls had spent many years living at Synanon, and though some things were different, such as the incredible order in the place, and the belief in such things as the game and moral ascendancy, they nevertheless were typical American teenagers worried about their looks and their boyfriends.

Though the Synanon woman was certainly liberated from the duties of child care, the rest of her goals were pretty traditional. In the words of a fifteen-year-old girl who had spent almost all her life at Synanon, "I would like to get married and have a kid. And I want my old man to be faithful to me. Growing up in a commune hasn't made me less possessive. I feel jealousy and possessiveness. Lots of people here do. I think it's just part of human nature." The women were also involved in looking good. They all wore makeup, and the bathrooms were stocked with every cosmetic and hygienic product imaginable, and the women were often put down in games for being fat or sloppy.

There were many overweight people at Synanon, something we hadn't seen at any other commune. Maybe it was because the entire Synanon community had given up smoking, but whatever the reason, Synanon was more involved with food than just having its three squares a day. The dining room was always open, and people could get peanut butter and jelly sandwiches day or night, as well as ice cream, tea, coffee or soft drinks, or Fritos. The walls of the dining room were lined with boxes and cans of prepared food much the way public school lunchrooms are decorated with the Pilgrims' first harvest at Thanksgiving time.

Synanon's awareness of its own abundance did not stop with the food. Every child said how rich Synanon was, how it owned one and a half million dollars of vehicles and was about to buy new dairy equipment that cost nine thousand dollars. Like a collective rich kid, they told about how they got the best education and medical care possible, and as ultimate proof of their wealth they said that at Synanon they had lots of leisure time. "Man, where else could we have it this good!"

Synanon believes in progress on every level. In one of the Synanon pamphlets the question is asked, "What do we require to ensure our goal of success for our children?" and the answer given: "In a word, professionalism." Synanon believes so profoundly in its professionalism, and the progress it makes in human development, that it expects the children to "skip the stage of unlearning" that most people have to go through in order to grow up. This unlearning stage, which for most people means the loss of innocence, and an understanding of where they have been, is not seen as a positive situation at Synanon. Rather it means a time when the children would lose their faith and trust in Synanon, and the orderly progress would be retarded and confused. If the children are to reach the highest goals, they must be instructed by people trained in those areas, and the professionals help train the child until she or he, too, becomes professional, and then Synanon as a whole can progress to other stages of wealth and technology. The children live with the idea of progress. They move from one structured set of experiences to the next, one house to the next; each stage goes to the next level of growth, each child feeling proud as he moves ahead. Synanon is very future-oriented. Anger is delayed until a game can take place, sex is delayed until a girl reaches the legal age, rewards come only after hard work. The children point to Synanon's new buildings and future building sites much like the Israelis who live on the edge of the Negev point to their gardens and grass where once it was all desert.

Not only do the children live with a sense of progress, they get to see it in the lives of the Synanon people themselves. Each day, the children are reminded of reclaimed humanity as the boot-campers march by. They are the latest recruitment of drug addicts to arrive at Synanon. They live apart from the rest of the community in army tents, and one sees them only as they march by on their way to work (they do all shit labor at Synanon).

They chant as they go by, the men with shaven heads, the women with untidy hair. They wear grubby old clothes and big ugly shoes, and they all seem to have pimples and sullen faces. But the children know they won't always be like that. They have seen it before. Within a few months these boot-campers will have kicked their habit. Their pimples will disappear and soon they will be able to move into men's and women's dorms and become a part of the Synanon community, clean and neat and with a smile for everyone. If Synanon didn't make it a practice for them to play their tapes, one would never guess at their origin.

Ex-drug addicts are constantly reminding themselves and each other how bad it used to be, and how good it is now. A girl named Abby, seventeen years old, the same age as the Finishing School girls, played her tapes for us.

"I came here three years ago, when I was fourteen. I was a personality disorder. That's what they call anyone who is a dope fiend or drinks, anyone who isn't a square or a lifestyler. I got very depressed when I was younger, and started taking pills. My schoolwork went down and I started taking heroin and then I tried to kill myself. I turned myself in to Synanon and it took me about a year to pull myself together. Then I met Ron. He came in as a lifestyler and we wanted to get married. I was still pretty young and not really that far from being a character disorder, but I guess they were impressed by the way I handled myself so they gave us permission to get married [they being the board of regents]. Now Ron and I live together and I work in the medical laboratory. They are planning to start a college here, and I would love to be able to go and study theory but I might have to work instead, because they might not want to put all that money and energy into a character disorder. There's far more chance that a lifestyler kid would be able to go to a school like that. But I would be willing to work and go to school even though it would be very hard."

We asked her if she would leave Synanon if she didn't get the chance to go to the school.

"Of course not. I would understand that at that time it just couldn't be. We believe in containment here. That is not getting everything you want, but working and hoping for it, and then quite often it comes. One time everybody here wanted to go to the movies on the weekends, but it was just too expensive, and too much of a hassle, so we didn't go but we thought about it a lot. Then, a few months later, some friend of someone's called and said he was going to donate a projector and send a Hollywood film once a week."

"But isn't it unfair that distinctions are made between junkies and lifestylers?"

"No. You see, there is no distinction made between the kid of a lifestyler and the kid of a junkie, just between the lifestyler and junkie. After all, a lifestyler comes in as a healthy person and puts his money and energy into Synanon, while the junkie is just using it up. There are distinctions the other way round, though. If a junkie gets money from home and doesn't share it, well, nobody really minds. But if a lifestyler who pledges his money to Synanon welches, well, he might be in trouble. If a lifestyler decides to leave, well, we are sad, but after all it was his free choice to come in the first place. But if a dope fiend leaves that's really bad. I would never talk to them again. I mean I would never try to contact them on the street and I think I would have a hard time being friends with them if they ever came back. Splittees are very debilitating to the group. Synanon puts so much work and money and love into the dope fiend, I think he owes it to the next person who needs help to stick around."

"Aren't you very young to be married?"

"Well, I guess so, but it's the only way to have sex around here at my age. The legal age for a girl to go down in California is eighteen, and if some of our neighbors who are always trying to make trouble for us heard we were getting it on before that we could get into a lot of trouble, maybe lose a lot of our benefactors, and maybe even our tax status. Sex is very important here. We don't smoke or drink or take drugs, so that's what we do, and talk about. And of course, for companionship. There are really no pressures here to get married, and also Chuck doesn't believe that marriage has to be forever, just so long as it's legal while it lasts, and so long as he believes the couple getting married is mature enough to handle it."

"How do you handle the problems of marriage?"

"In the game, of course. You can't say personal negative things outside the game. If someone said them to me, I would be very upset. I couldn't take it. But in a game there are other people around, who sort of moderate, or at least take the weight off and I won't take it as a personal criticism."

Listening to Abby, we can get an idea of how Synanon transforms a social misfit into a highly socialized person. The goal at Synanon is for all its members to be highly socialized, and that is a good goal for the various cripples who make their home there. But what about the children who grow up there? Their possibilities seem to be severely limited to achieving just this kind of socialization and nothing more. They did not come to Synanon with personality disorders, and yet their lives are as structured as if they in fact needed this kind of custodial care. They have grown dependent on a game that is an important crutch for the personality disorder. They are afraid of the outside world; they share the same emotions as the people who have once been sick, though they themselves have never been sick. Synanon seems ultimately to treat its addicts and children alike.

❦ 8 ❧

The Farm

"We live closer to our kids than square folks do. And we ain't got bedrooms to put them in and stuff, doors and stuff, mostly. And we got to work it out with them pretty much. It was a change when we moved into our busses because we used to just stick Martha in the front room and let her yell. Close the door and turn on the radio. But we couldn't do that in the bus, so we worked it out with her. And just in the last few months she's getting over a tendency to rip us off a little every morning. We've had a lot of other kids staying with us and she's been embarrassed to hogan (to goof off) in front of them. . . ."

Stephen Gaskin
The Farm

The Farm is the communards' commune. From the Ozarks all the way to California they talk about it. People who know first-hand how hard it is to get along with twenty other people marvel at the six hundred adults and two hundred children who have spent more than five years at the Farm without killing each

169

other. On almost every commune bookshelf, among the how-to books, you find a copy of *Monday Night Class,* the teachings of Steve Gaskin, founder of the Farm, and recognized as the most eloquent spokesman for the commune way of life. You also find people arguing vehemently about whether it is a good thing that six hundred Farm members have chosen to listen to Gaskin and follow his teachings.

One thing everyone agrees about: the Farm knows how to raise children. Not only its own two hundred children, but the Farm is famous for having a powerful reforming effect on outsiders' children. In several communes, there were people who had visited the Farm with whiny, bitchy children on their hands and then left two days later with quiet, polite children. These miracles are so legendary that more than fifty people a day arrive at the gates of the Farm, in the hills of western Tennessee, on some sort of behavioral pilgrimage.

We wouldn't have paid so much attention to these stories if the same thing hadn't happened to us—by pure accident. Being in Tennessee, the Farm was one of the first scheduled stops on our trip; we stumbled onto it unaware of its importance, like backing into the Taj Mahal. Chauncey and Bernsie were whiny, bitchy children, to be sure; they were acting so bad that we had to consider scrapping the trip. But we never once considered that the Farm people, or any other commune people, could possibly say or do anything that would affect how a sophisticated urban couple like us handles children. So we didn't even come for the cure, and yet, four days later, we left just like the rest—marveling at our two well-behaved companions, totally transformed in our theories of parenthood, carrying Gaskin messages in our heads and Gaskin tapes in the trunk of our car, extolling the Farm virtures to every other person we met for the next several months.

Even if you haven't been zapped by the Farm, the sheer numbers of its population and size are mind-boggling. All these people gave up professional careers to live in voluntary poverty and eat soybeans and get up at 4:30 A.M. at the sound of primitive shell horns to go to work. The place has not shrunk since 1968; it has grown. Very few originals have left; they have been joined by over one hundred newcomer adults on this eleven-hundred-acre tract. Since the Farm does not practice birth control, the few babies who arrived in 1968 have been joined by more than one hundred fifty others in a rising tide of children. As far as Steve Gaskin is concerned, there cannot be too many children at the Farm. He even encourages women who are about to have abortions to go ahead and have the children and give them to the Farm. He wants as many people as possible to grow up in this new culture.

The way the originals got here is a motorized version of the Mormon trek, and someday it will probably be understood in the same terms. It began in San Francisco at the height of the college turbulence when Steve Gaskin, a favored disciple of S. I. Hayakawa at San Francisco State, and headed for a successful academic career, dropped out, took a lot of drugs, and then gave up the drugs and began to lecture on how to get naturally high, how to live high without LSD. It was the same message, essentially, that many traditional revival preachers had adopted to try to reach the youth market, but with Gaskin it was different. He had tried the drugs, for one thing, and he had given up on career America, for another. He wasn't selling any packaged religious principle, just a search for a new way of life. His Monday night classes, as his lectures were called, were attended by more than five hundred people in San Francisco, many of the same people who ended up with Gaskin in Tennessee. They were mostly students and professionals who were also expected to become successful at something, but somehow Gaskin was able to lead them away from it. He got them to outfit thirty-five or forty old school busses, painted in bright swirls, and head out across the country in a hippie hegira. After a year of roaming around, picking up converts, they settled on a piece of land in Tennessee, pooled all their remaining money, and bought it. Here were former lawyers and physicists and English majors and bureaucrats, living in the busses, in army tents, trying to scratch a subsistence living from soybean farming. It might have been a short-term vacation from professional pressures, like joining the Peace Corps, but after six or seven years of living in the busses and the tents, you have to believe them when they say the Farm is their lifetime commitment.

You can see all the busses and tents in front of you in the middle of a hefty chunk of farmland, but they don't just let you drive in. They stop you at the gate, a military-looking outpost with a small black telephone and a sign-in sheet and several people standing around. We also went through a kind of gate with the Synanon people, who wanted to know our credentials on paper, and when they accepted us on paper, then they let us in. We took that as Synanon's hang-up on experts; none of the less formal communes had a screening process; they didn't care who we were, they just invited us to stay on friendliness alone. That's what stopped us short when the Farm people told us to get out of our car at Checkpoint Charlie: they looked like hang-loose hippies, they said "far out" and "groovy," they came on with nonchalance, and yet it was clear they weren't going to let us in. A Farm lady named Melanie, wearing a nineteenth-century-style granny dress, which is what all the Farm women wore, and a Farm man named Michael, with a long pony tail and Oshkosh overalls and one of the pants legs pinned up where a leg was missing, kept giving us searching stares. They hung around us at the little outpost, Susan and Chauncey and Berns and me standing by the car, and didn't answer my questions about when we could go in and where we could pitch a tent.

It seemed there was plenty of room to pitch a tent; beyond the gate was nothing but old busses and army surplus tents far out to the horizon. There was also no lack of people. There were all ages in there: toddlers and waddlers, kids on tricycles, teenagers, and farmers in their middle twenties, all wearing long dresses or overalls, wandering the dirt footpaths with the air of a bonus army camping out in a wheatfield. I didn't see how our presence could be that important or unimportant to eight hundred people, but Michael kept saying he wasn't ready to let us in.

I tried everything to soften him up with a reference to our being writers (maybe they liked publicity?) but that hardened him. Then a reference to our not *really* being like other writers—"We're here for the experience, not the information"—but that didn't impress him, either. As we stood there longer, my own version of our purpose was reduced to: "We're just traveling around, really, just trying to find out what's happening." Michael wasn't interested. The only thing he said, beyond refusing to open the gates, was, "I'm not getting telepathic with Susan." Susan up to this time hadn't uttered a single word.

It was clear that words were not what they wanted. We were being put through a test, but it was not like any other test either of us had ever been asked to pass. Whatever they wanted certainly was not verbal, not like it was in the Jesus-freak places where they would ask, "Are you in Jesus?" and you could say yes and then nothing else mattered. And it was not a credential check like Synanon's, where you could flash your ego trip and the doors would open. Michael and Melanie weren't listening to anything we said, they were standing there *feeling* us, much as a dog sniffs out a visitor for fear. It made both of us very uncomfortable, this telepathic probe. Communes in general existed in a nonrational spirit world, but nowhere else had being high been tacked onto an entrance examination. People have been refused service on grounds of race and religion, but we had never been refused on grounds of vibes. Michael and Melanie were playing a waiting game, waiting to pin something on our spirits.

They got their chance with the children. Chauncey and Bernsie were obnoxiously tugging at Susan's skirt, which Susan was trying to ignore like any grownup who is attempting to deal with other grownups. Nothing too serious, but Melanie seemed personally offended; she launched into a speech about how could we judge other people's children when ours were so pushy and demanding. To Susan she said, "Your kids are ripping you off a whole bunch, don't you ever say no to your kids?" Susan parried this impolite intrusion with some kind of mumbled remark about its being hard to travel with kids, but Melanie kept hammering at her until Susan got red around the ears. If it hadn't been for the journalistic gold mine just on the other side of the gate, we would have told the sentries to go fuck themselves and gotten back in the car. But then with what I thought was remarkable tact, Susan just shrugged her shoulders and said, "I was just being defensive.

Wouldn't you be if two strangers suddenly jumped down your throat?" Michael and Melanie laughed, and that remark, that submission, opened the gate. Michael said, "I think you can take four days." An odd choice of words; it sounded like that's how long he calculated we could stand the place without cracking up.

"And what keeps a community from being stoned together is the individual members ripping each other off so bad that nobody can get on. That's what makes this a pretty stoned community is that we have spoken openly about people ripping energy off of people so much that everybody knows how it works. And everybody sees it ain't as easy to do as it used to be. It used to be pretty easy to rip people off, 'cause people didn't know they're being ripped off or what it was. And kids gotta learn that stuff from grownups."

Steve Gaskin

We left the gate still unsure of what hit us, but glad it was over. The relief lasted for about two minutes. The first building beyond the gate was the Farm school, and we stopped there long enough for several dozen children to rush the car as if it were a broken piñata, pinning us against the door and asking for candy, gum, toys. It was the movie version of the American GI besieged by urchins in the war zone. They seemed as desperate to see a visitor who might give them something as Melanie and Michael had been reluctant to let us in, and our car was a moving temptation to them. Maybe that was part of Michael and Melanie's reluctance; everything else around us, the tractors, the tents, the simple clothes, and no jewelry of any kind, looked incredibly gray and sparse. Melanie would not permit the children the joy of a momentary fantasy that our portable suburb represented; she gave the children basically the same talk she had given us at the gate: "Why are you ripping off these visitors? You know not to cop to this scene. Get away from here."

The Farm children immediately obeyed Melanie, and we got back in the car, the only car on a road full of bicycles and walking people and an unbelievable tranquillity that must have existed everywhere before the automobile. It was like driving through an underdeveloped country, really, you could feel the serenity right through the windshield, but you couldn't help feeling sorry for all those kids without gum and candy. Not, of course, connecting the coming of the gum and the candy with the end of the serenity. We tried to ask Melanie about the physical deprivation of Farm children (why else would they have been so excited by a few trinkets?) but Melanie seemed only interested in Bernsie and Chauncey as behavioral problems. That tells you the difference between us and the Farm right off the bat—we worried about their kids' assets, they worried about our kids' character. Melanie zoomed right in on Bernsie just as she had done with Susan at the gate.

Bernsie, it is true, was going through a particularly obnoxious stage of her life—back in Miami the other mothers with similar daughters called it the Terrible Twos. Berns would whine, cry, and go through an elaborate ritual of falling down and insisting she had a broken leg. She wouldn't get up until someone agreed to carry her. A command performance, which we always went along with, because we didn't know what else to do. It seemed easier to carry the star offstage than to leave her crying on the ground. Besides, it was something to joke about with other parents whose children were going through equally obnoxious routines. But Melanie would not have it. I don't know why she even cared—Berns had nothing to do with her—but when we got out of the car and Berns went into the broken-leg number, Melanie said, in what was becoming familiar Farm language, "We don't cop to that behavior," and took Berns back to the car, ushered her inside, and told her, "Don't come out until you shape up." Nobody had ever done that to Berns. We were stunned. It was one thing for this woman to comment on Susan's permissiveness, but now she had taken control of the children and was using our car as a prison. At best, it was a totally impetuous intrusion on our parental rights, and at worst, it was an emotional kidnaping. But Melanie was so sure of herself that for some reason we went along with it and walked away from the car. Back through the windshield, you could see Berns, revving up for one of her major tantrums.

The tantrum never really got off the ground, because Berns gave in to the Farm just as we were doing. A few minutes of minor-league whimpering, and Berns was out of the car and by our side, walking under her own power. She tried falling down once again, just to test the opposition, and when Melanie moved for her, she immediately got up and that's the last we ever saw of that particular performance. Our outrage at this meddling Farm woman was softened with a little admiration, because she had accomplished in five minutes what seemed to us to be a major development; we viewed it as a miracle, really, as miraculous as a child originally learning to walk. "As long as you are unsure of yourself with your children," Melanie said, "they'll rip you off. You gotta get straight with them." And she left us standing in a subdivision of old school busses.

Despite her gift as a child-trainer, we were not sorry to see Melanie go. There was something snippy and constantly unsettling about her, and we were glad that our case was being turned over to David and Patricia. David and Patricia are a typical Farm couple; the word that they constantly suggest is robust. They give off a healthy glow that you associate with Benjamin Franklin clichés. They came right out to help us pitch a tent next to their Bluebird school bus, which was part of a neighborhood that included a Greyhound travelcruiser, a small camper, a minibus (where David and Patricia's children lived), a couple of army tents built up on wooden platforms, and a two-seater outhouse that they called the "shitter." In terms of possessions, the Farm was by far the poorest place we visited; they were right down with the shack squatters, really—David and Patricia had a bed and a few pillows in their bus, a copy of Steve Gaskin's book, a kerosene lamp, some pots and pans, and old clothes. Since coming to the Farm in 1968, they had given all their money to the community and now they had to struggle along with everybody else to keep enough soybeans on the table. The Farm diet, while we were there, consisted of soybean gruel, soybean cakes, soybean patties, and even soybean coffee. The only relief from the soybeans was some wild greens picked right from the ground by the children during the afternoons. We understood why the children had rushed the car.

The first evening in David and Patricia's bus, we all sat on the bed and smoked a few joints (which at the Farm they called their "sacrament") and talked about the Farm. It was one of the only times anyone discussed their personal lives with us at the Farm. David, who was about twenty-seven years old, said he had been a postal clerk in Washington, D.C., and was not liking it much. He was seeing Patricia at the time; she was a divorced woman, in her early thirties, with two children, Lois and Glenna. Patricia said she "spent most of my time wearing hot pants and ripping off men." Both attended a Gaskin lecture when he came through town, and like dozens of other people in similar situations, they got on the bus. They were married by Gaskin, and hadn't left the Farm in five years. Since coming here, Patricia had another child, who slept in a crib in the end of the bus. Her two older children occupied their own mini-bus, which was backed up to the end of the big bus like a caboose.

I couldn't understand how David and Patricia could possibly prefer this soybean austerity and bus-stop living to whatever they had had before. But both of them said they loved it here. What's more, they looked like they loved it here. Poor but happy. It is unfashionable now to believe that poor people can actually lead more joyous lives than rich people anywhere in the world; we are accustomed to dismissing that view as an apology for poverty. "They just think they are happy now," we say of the Cuna Indians and other primitive tribes, "but wait and ask them after they buy their first television." And yet David and Patricia had given up television and cars and the balanced meal and everything else that we pity the rest of the world for not yet having. Sitting on the bed in their bus, we began to feel threatened by their total acceptance of the Farm way of life. We could have felt threatened in other communes, among other people who had also given up more things in favor of a better life, but at the Farm, the implied comparison between their way and ours came to the surface.

They lived much poorer than the other commune people we had visited, and also they had a clearer notion of why their existence, for all its austerity, was superior to ours.

"And if you don't teach kids how to be, they'll just all learn. What they learn is random, whatever strikes their fancy. On a system of what looks together. Or what's amusing. Or what might be fun this week."

Steve Gaskin

The conversation with David and Patricia was another version of what happened at the Farm gate. We were interested in their apparent poverty; they were interested in the apparent poverty of our behavior. It kept getting around to Chauncey and Bernsie again—Chauncey would squirm up on my lap while I was talking to David, like Chauncey always did, and David would put Chauncey outside the bus for "ripping me off." The next time around, made aware by David that Chauncey's squirming did make me uncomfortable, I would yell at Chauncey to get off the bus. Then David would correct *me,* saying, "You shouldn't get angry. Anger is a very heavy thing for a kid to deal with." And it was true, we never did see a Farm person get angry. It was obvious that they just did not accept what we considered to be normal behavior, either of squirming children or huffy grownups. The ordeal at the gate had not been an idle attempt to throw us off guard, it was a proof that our spirits and our whole way of being was inferior to the Farm way of being. They let us in only on the chance that we could be uplifted, much the way the first black was let into Yale. Apparently, we required correction at every turn. David said our not being straight with the children just interrupted our "feeling groovy."

"Feeling groovy" was how David and Patricia explained their staying at the Farm. They gave all that other stuff up not for some abstract notion of utopia, but for that very specific euphoria that comes when you are stoned and in love with the world. It was a state they tried to reach not with drugs (except for their "sacrament," which was only a reminder of what they were working toward) but by following a rigid code of behavior developed by Steve Gaskin. As we walked with David and Patricia around the Farm in the quiet of the evening (no sounds but from a couple of tractors working twenty-four hours a day), we passed by the people and sensed an eerie unity among them. I tried to pinpoint the feeling, among all these farmers and carpenters and children riding bicycles to the communal showers, and saw that it had to do with how they used their eyes. They would focus in on each other, from as far as two hundred yards away, staring into each other's eyes with the intensity of airport homing beacons, not kicking out until that person had passed and another was picked up on the screen. If you don't think that kind of constant staring affects the spirit of a place, try it for a day or two in your home or office and see how long people can stand it. David said it was all part of being telepathic. And it's true: the vibrations were so uniform, and so alien to us, that the one person we picked out among the crowd as somebody we could possibly talk to turned out to be a tormented city person who had only arrived at the Farm a few days earlier. That's who we were telepathic with.

Telepathy was a growing thing with them. The unity here was, according to Steve Gaskin, only a first step—things could get much cozier and tighter than they were now. Gaskin recognized people's limitations, people who just came out of Western civilization; he started them out slowly on the path of complete communalism. Take marriage. Farm people were strict believers in marriage; single people were kept isolated by sex, premarital sex was discouraged, extramarital sex was anathema. Most people at the Farm were married, by Gaskin himself, in a meadow on the back part of the property. The commitment part of marriage was important—the Farm people did not believe in idle screwing around—but the traditional form of the marriage was only a beginning step. From the basic two-marriage, Farm people who felt ready for it could move into a four-marriage, four people together, switching partners, with the same seriousness and commitment as the regular arrangement. Not everybody could han-

179

dle a four-marriage right away, Gaskin recognized that—there were only a handful of such marriages at the Farm. Then, for a few people of great ability, there were six-marriages (Gaskin himself is in one of those) and presumably, so on up the line, until you have a six-hundred-marriage, which I think is Gaskin's ultimate goal. Get everybody as close together as a husband and wife can be. But the six-hundred-marriage is a long way off; the hope for that lies not with the original Farm pioneers—who grew up with too much selfishness—but with the new Farm children.

We stopped in on a four-marriage that occupies the Greyhound bus next to David and Patricia. Sabrina, a five-year-old, is a daughter of this marriage, and when we first met her she said, "My daddies and my mommies got pissed today." When we asked her what it was like to have two fathers, she said, "Oh, I have three. My real daddy doesn't live here. But he comes to visit when the moon is full."

Sabrina lives with her real mother and her new mother and two new fathers in a giant bus. She was, of course, born outside the four-marriage, but her two sisters, two and three years old, were born into it. The children sleep on foam mattresses on the floor, while the parents switch between two double beds. When we visited the bus, only Sabrina's mother Greta was home; the rest of the marriage was out working.

Susan: Are the babies your children?

Greta: One of them is.

Susan: Can you tell which husband is the actual father?

Greta: Not for sure. But we think we know.

Susan: Can the children tell?

Greta: No, but I don't think it matters to them. They just have two fathers.

Susan: What about mothers?

Greta: Well, they do know their biological mother, but they don't act differently to one of us than to the other. They don't act differently to any of the Farm people.

Susan: What about Sabrina?

Greta: It is harder for her, coming from a regular family. But she's getting along.

Farm people hardly ever talked. That's another general impression of all the communes that was part of the code of the Farm: talk was not valued. Talk was not a way of becoming telepathic, at one with the group; it interrupted whatever surreal contact all those eyes were making, the flow of the vibes. They talked at the Farm only to work out a problem; talk was like the sound of the pickax against the rocks when you are climbing the mountain. When you are on top of the mountain, no sound is necessary. They *had* to talk to us because we were a problem, our vibes weren't connected, and so we got a heavy dose of Farm language.

The language of the Farm is remarkably homogeneous. You hear the same expressions, the same inflections, from Melanie and David and Patricia and the hundreds of other people who seemed to jump from behind trees to tell us off. "Ripped off," "ripping off your juice," "being groovy," "copping to behavior" —we heard it so often that we began to suspect the same tape recorder was running through six hundred heads. David confirmed the suspicion; he said all the words came from Steve Gaskin. Not only the general ideas, but the exact words, sentences, and even paragraphs, were taken from the prophet's mouth and directly transfused into the brains of every other Farm person. There was no need to attribute the quotes to Gaskin, it was just assumed that the best way a Farm person could use his mind was to store Gaskin messages. That left the person free of his own thoughts, free to be telepathic.

Every Sunday, Gaskin gave a sermon, an extension of his old Monday night class, which the Farm people would not only hear live, but listen to again and again on tape recorders until they had it down. The weekend we were there, people had a choice of traveling to Nashville to hear Gaskin speak in person, or congregating in the Farm barn, where they could hear Gaskin speak on tape. One of the tapes floating around happened to be Gaskin's statement on raising children, and we were naturally anxious to hear the philosophy behind the diffuse criticisms we had been getting. The crux of it was this:

"If a kid's ripping off a bunch of folks, lots of times I see a kid ripping off a whole bunch of grownups, and his parents won't do anything about it 'cause they don't want to leave the scene. ('Oh, I'll miss something, I won't know what's going on.') But if every time a kid opened his mouth at a meeting, you just picked him up and walked him away from the energy center, then he'd get to where he wouldn't have to do that every time. He'd shut up so he could stay where the action was. But like it requires you getting up and walking out of earshot of the meeting . . .

"Here's the thing. It ain't a question of how you do it, but of understanding what you're trying to do. And like what you're trying to do is not to teach your kid to be a rip-off. Because if somebody gets to be a rip-off, they can keep it up for the rest of their life. Like Edward, you know (a grownup who lives at the Farm). Edward learned to be a rip-off when he was a little kid. And you see kids learn to do that.

"We were in a park in Meridian watching the scene and there was this one cat jiving through and he never moved ordinary, all the time it was snapping fingers, and he never talked nothing but jive. And nobody knew what he was talking about and he'd come up and lean on you and put his arm around your neck and just jive on you—just a stoned rip-off. And like that cat don't know what subconscious is and he's a walking lump of it. And he don't know nothing about that and yet everything he does is some kind of an against-the-grain movement or gesture . . . just like an old hog scratching his back against the barbed-wire fence, this cat scratches himself against the reality of everyone around him. All the time for juice, for being a rip-off. And it's going to take something heavy for that cat [to change]. You know, he might have to blow his mind on a heavy psychedelic, or get busted, to snap him. And his folks taught him when he was a little kid by giving him juice when he was freaky, but not giving him juice for being groovy."

Gaskin's tape made it clearer what the Farm was trying to do. That man in Meridian was like all America, really, brought up by parents who rewarded him for stealing the show, for getting attention, for personal achievement. All the people who got on that Gaskin caravan now saw themselves as ex-energy-rip-offs, raised by parents to be part of a selfish culture, but now part of a groovier, unselfish one. David talked to us about his parents, how they didn't understand why he was living at the Farm, how they couldn't stop giving him things. "They think," he said, "that if they hadn't spoiled me so much as a child, I wouldn't be here now."

The Farm people had blown their minds on Gaskin and dropped out of America; they had to get over their selfishness, and they were going to spare their children that trouble. They were raising them from the beginning not to be rip-offs, not only not to steal things, but not to steal time, or attention, or extra praise. They had taken the informal desire of most commune parents to produce better-behaved children than suburban Americans produce, and turned it into a rigorous, all-out program.

There were two hundred Farm children, and they were hardly noticeable. At The Last Resort or at the Ranch, just a few children could, from time to time, completely monopolize the scene —but here the two hundred children were invisible. Lois (ten) and Glenna (four), who were Patricia's daughters, were typical of all of them—they came home from the Farm school and hung out in their minibus and would emerge for dinner in the classic "be seen and not heard" manner. When it was time to take a shower (and Lois and Glenna decided that on their own), they got a towel and soap and walked the two miles to the communal shower stalls without asking anybody. They had the same leeway to decide things as the Ranch children, but without the same sloppy results. Farm children always looked good—their clothes were old and patched, but in them they managed to look respectable.

During the day, they were not allowed to just hang out, but were organized into brigades. It was also true of the parents: at the sound of the shell horns, before the sun was up, the parents dispersed into various work crews all around the property. Work was the priority at the Farm, harvesting the soybeans and building houses out of salvage lumber. The babies were kept in Lincoln log cribs built into each communal building, so the mothers could watch them and work at the same time. The three- to five-year-olds were sent to the Kid Herd, a roving kindergarten watched over by only two people. The older children walked to the one-room schoolhouse, which was, incredibly enough, accredited by the state of Tennessee. It was the most satisfactory resolution of the school versus community problem that we had seen—the Farm had its school, right on the property, the teachers were Farm members, and the state gave its certification, even though marijuana was a publicized part of general Farm life, and even though the school only taught regular subjects for half a day. The other half was reserved for studying the thoughts of Steve Gaskin.

This was communalism taken to its ultimate conclusion. Not only were the adults interchangeable in their relations with the children, but the children themselves had become interchangeable. Susan worked with the Kid Herd during the morning while I went off with some carpenters—they wouldn't allow me to just wander around. There were about twenty little children, all of them sitting on the ground waiting for instructions, like the pictures you see of little children in Mao's China. This morning, they were going to build a small bridge across a stream. They worked together with their pieces of wood, all in perfect harmony, until this one kid broke away from the group and ran across the river, announcing that "I'm the first one across, you can't catch me." That one kid was Chauncey.

Chauncey and Bernsie stood out among the children as we stood out among the grownups. The only voice you could hear from all points of the property was Bernsie's. It was amazing, dozens of babies and toddlers sprinkled through all the buildings at the Farm, and yet we literally never heard a child crying. Children were walking up hills, pulling wagons, even as young as eighteen months old, but they were not crying. David told us it was because the Farm "put them out of the energy center when they cry." Putting children outside was their sure cure for everything.

When the Farm children did come on to us, as individual people, it was usually to correct us for something. They were not reluctant to intervene, just as Melanie had done. In fact, they used exactly the same terminology. Glenna, the little four-year-old daughter of Patricia, was always piping up with admonitions to Bernsie: "You shouldn't rip off your mother." "You shouldn't hogan [complain] so much." Sabrina, the five-year-old who lived in a neighboring Greyhound bus, told Chauncey not to call Susan "mommy" anymore. They didn't use possessive words at the Farm, and called everyone by his first name. In one day, Chauncey and Bernsie got into that habit, and still over a year later they don't call Susan "mommy."

The children ran the Gaskin tapes so much there was no room for personal discussion. In fact, after combing the place for three days, we found only one kid who would submit to an interview. That was Vincent, a teenager who had been at the Farm for about a year and kept running away or getting kicked out by Steve Gaskin. We met him at one of the army tents reserved for the single men; Vincent was outside waiting, a cocky kid who said we could ask him anything and then didn't even wait for us to ask. He sat us down on a log and began to ramble about all his exploits on the road, how he didn't get along with his father, how he got busted, how Gaskin kicked him out for screwing a woman in the showers. Telling this story on the steps of any high school in America, Vincent could have commanded quite an audience; he had us sitting there taking it all down. Yet the minute some Farm people came by and heard what was happening, they shut him down. "Hey, Vincent, get off your ego trip," one of them said. "You sound like a microphone is stuck in your throat." We explained that we were just interviewing him, and were told that "interviewing is rip-off behavior. There is work to be done." Using a lot of words on yourself was like stealing.

The power of this place was tremendous. They did not believe in violence, and even raising your voice was anathema here, and yet the children were totally socialized. Vincent was the only rebellious one. The rest were all part of the telepathic hum. Gaskin's success had to do with a complete lack of privacy. Physical privacy, of course, was unavailable—the single people lived in large communal tents and the married people lived in those big busses that were always full of people at night, and during the day they worked in the crews. They ate communally, took showers communally, and even shit communally, since each outhouse had two seats. (That was so disturbing to us that I went out at 2 A.M. to shit, and the first time I sat down on the toilet and a big hairy Farm person came over and sat right next to me, my sphincter shriveled up in protest.)

But physical privacy was the least of it. There was the lack of emotional privacy, all those eyes staring at you for the slightest sign of torment, all those hundreds of people jumping out to correct you for any rip-off behavior. When I hit my thumb with a hammer and yelled out "Fuck," the man next to me came over and said, "You shouldn't yell like that. That's a very heavy reaction for the little thing that happened to you." Susan was admonished so many times not to coddle Bernsie that once, when Bernsie ambled onto a path and was knocked down on the ground by a bicycle, Susan suppressed all her motherly instinct and left Berns lying there—for fear of being accused of letting Berns rip her off.

After one day, we were driven back into our tent by the constant nagging. I quit the carpentry crew, claiming exhaustion (which was true). Susan couldn't face returning to the Kid Herd. Chauncey and Bernsie were continually stunned by what was happening to them. It was total cultural shock. Our tent was the only ten-foot-square space on the entire eleven hundred acres of property where Farm vibrations did not reach. There we could sneer and make cynical remarks and not worry if Chauncey knocked over a lantern. "We don't look too good on their turf," I said. "I wonder how they look on ours." Their children, I meant. We wanted to get some of them inside our nuclear outpost to test the strength of the Farm against the corrupting power of a rip-off family.

The second afternoon, when school was over, Susan got out some raisins, the only bribe we could safely offer their kids since the parents were strict vegetarians and also against candy. Remembering the reception at the portable suburb, Susan went outside down the path and lured Glenna and Sabrina and another neighborhood five-year-old into the tent. Berns and Chauncey, of course, were there, too. We had three boxes of raisins for four girls, and Bernsie immediately asked for her own box. Glenna and Sabrina, following her lead, said they wanted special boxes, and so did the other little girl. That brought on a terrible fight. There were raisins flying and threats to tell parents and pulling and tugging and all manner of behavior that had been totally absent up to now. Five minutes back into America and it was every little girl for herself.

Things like that happened several times in or around our tent. Not just fighting, but shoving and game-playing and general playground behavior. Bernsie had a lot of other girls grabbing for her dolls. Chauncey got Lois in several arguments over which games they would play. Small stuff, but enough to make us feel vindicated—like, their kids can be human, too.

I suggested that to David and he told me I was wrong. "Kids react to the energy that's around them," he said. "They pick up whatever's there. It's no surprise that with you, they act a certain way. They pick that up. That's why we spread visitors around, because it's hard to integrate that energy. After we get a visitor, it takes us a couple of days to get straight again."

And it's true, we did put out different vibes. Aggressive, inquisitive ego vibes. For one thing, we were writers. There were no writers at the Farm, no artists or thinkers or people who pursued their own projects. All that private stuff, it interfered with the real work of the Farm and it interfered with telepathy. David told an amazing story about how the community made its choices: there was a doctor at the Farm, and with all those people the place certainly needed one, and he was willing to set up practice right there inside the gates. But this particular man, David said, was on an ego trip about how important it was that he was a doctor. Well, that's just what we have to put up with, I said, the ego trip is part of the training to be a doctor. What doctor isn't a little like that? But David told me the Farm would not permit this man to practice, he had to be a farmer; it was more important to them that he straighten out his head than that he use his skill in an impure way.

The Farm was not interested in producing successful people like that. In fact, you could go down a list of the hundred most important Americans from Gerald Ford to Ralph Nader to Gloria Steinem, and I doubt if any of them would even be allowed past the gates. The Farm is so far away from that, that the people we call the best and the brightest are to them just examples of pathetic emotional cripples. And you could see it beginning right with the children—we were teaching Chauncey and Bernsie to be inquisitive and judgmental and pushy, and to value the extra attention they receive, while the Farm children were learning just the opposite qualities. When Susan began reading *Alice's Adventures in Wonderland* to a group of them, and Sabrina asked a question about some word she didn't understand, Patricia chastised Sabrina for interrupting the story. It was more important that a child learn not to interrupt than that she learn some new fact or concept.

What is the Farm trying to produce in its two hundred children? David said it simply: "We take seriously what our parents *said*, as opposed to what they *did*." In other words, they were trying to produce moral children, children who believe in marriage and keeping quiet and not lying and working hard and helping their neighbors. In many aspects Farm parents were strait-laced in a way reminiscent of the nineteenth century—while we were there, Lois, who was ten, was taken before the entire community and criticized for doing some sexual experimentation with a Farm boy about her age. Farm children were strictly forbidden to experiment with sex, even though they often saw their parents fucking (living in busses, how could they avoid seeing?). They watched their parents smoke grass, but were not allowed to participate in that, either—Chauncey was so used to taking a puff that he was quite upset when David told him he was "showing off." Patricia said the reason for the double standard was that kids "should have room to be kids and not be saddled with a lot of heavy trips that they can't handle."

Room to be kids. It seemed, on the bottom line, that that was exactly what Farm children did not have. They could not express anger, they could not play games. Their own emotions were the china dishes and Chippendale chairs of the middle-class living room, not to be played on, not to be misused. Their lives were like an elaborate karate exercise, where every gesture, every breath, every look was counted by the eyes of the community, scrutinized and paid attention to. I suspect the Farm is the most tightly controlled culture in the world. Steve Gaskin would say it is the most aware culture.

The same strictures, of course, existed for the adults, and we were strangled in them. It was incredible to think of these people as having voluntarily left America for this place—their lives were changed as drastically as the Cuban middle class would have been changed had it stayed in Cuba under Fidel. As drastically as the traditional Chinese family was changed by Mao.

We could have been reporters, covering this bizarre culture like the teams that have recently visited China, and returning with the simple verdict: "They are different from us." But there was Chauncey and Bernsie to consider. They were the key to our stay at the Farm. If it had not been for them, we might have been more severe in our judgments—about how the Farm people have given up their individuality, about how their children are so many prisoners to Steve Gaskin. I don't know what the result would be if a Chinese worker grabbed the child of a U.S. cameraman and said, "Hey, man, your kid is on an ego trip," but in our case, the results were staggering. After four days of struggle, Bernsie had begun to stop whining so much. Chauncey wasn't squirming and pushing for attention like a superstar so much. And more important, our awareness had been so extended by the Farm that we no longer accepted rip-off behavior as a natural part of childhood. From then on, when Bernsie whined, we stopped the car by the side of the road and made her get out of the energy center. It was difficult at first. But it began to work. Bernsie didn't hate us for it, she seemed generally less tormented.

That is the ultimate challenge of the Farm. Most Americans, for all their sophistication, somehow continue to believe that what is produced in their children is a natural sequence of childhood, beyond their control. The Farm people showed us (to our horror) how much a reflection of our own values Chauncey and Bernsie actually were. We could not help noticing that Farm children acted much better, seemed much more relaxed, much more under control. I thought of Miami, how little we saw of the children, and the thousand alien vibrations that passed through their heads every day. If they couldn't rip us off (which of course they could) there was always somebody else to rip off. At the Farm there was no chance to slip back.

Sunday was the communal day at the Farm, when they all go to the meadow at four-thirty to watch the sun come up and listen to Steve Gaskin. We deposited the children in the nearest Greyhound (they weren't allowed at the meeting) and walked to the meadow. Everyone converged there, all smiling and weekend clean. Farm people were walking with their parents, who had come in for a Sunday visit; you could tell the parents by their cameras and straw hats and leather handbags; they looked like American tourists—except the foreigners were their own sons and daughters.

There was a jubilant expectancy in the air, and we began to feel very stoned—it's the closest we came to being telepathic. Maybe because the children weren't around for the moment to remind us of who we were—we could pretend to lose our egos.

Everyone sat on the grass in silence until some person on the far end of the field started chanting "Om." Other people picked it up and the "om" went through the six hundred, back and forth, like electricity through a wet golfer. You could feel the air almost crackling. I could see what they meant by energy, the people-energy was mind-blowing.

Finally, a bearded man dressed in a simple shirt and blue jeans, no robes or trappings, got up to address the group. He was slight and ascetic-looking, in his late thirties, and by the hush that came over the crowd you knew it was Gaskin. Even before he spoke, I could finally understand his role here—it was like the conductor and the orchestra changing places. This whole mass of people was putting the energy into him, and he was making the music. He married two couples, and made a short speech that wasn't as good as what we had heard on tape. But the reality of what he had put together, these six hundred professionals working without pay, was truly staggering. I thought of Timothy Leary, the prophet of the 1960s, who began with drugs and ended with drugs, a broken man, and a shattered dream; and then of Gaskin, who used drugs to blow out of America and then discovered community, who transcended drugs into some kind of civilization. Gaskin himself had said: "Acid is a rocket ship and peyote is an oxcart, but it's only two miles to town." He and the other Farm people had definitely made it to town.

But we had to reconcile our admiration for the Farm with our anxiousness to get out of there. All the elevation was too much, really, the constant confrontation made us nervous to the point where we couldn't have taken another day of it. The gatekeeper was exactly right, four days was what we could handle. We were so spooked, actually, that we wondered if they were going to let us out. Can you accept what the Farm did to Chauncey and Bernsie, and yet not accept the Farm? I suppose it is a little like seeing the miracle and then turning down the religion, but we wanted to get back to our egos, our judgments, and our agonies. When we got through the gate, Susan and I both let out a simultaneous shriek that had been hiding out in us for four long days.

Conclusion

There are many different kinds of rural communes, but the thing
that unifies all of them is the behavior of the children. Mickey
Peyote visited the Farm and hated the place; he got sick of soybeans and tractors and telepathy and he resented living under a
dictator's yoke. The whole network of Colorado–New Mexico
communes, the people who are proud to be disorganized, the
macho factions, railed against the rigidity of places like the
Farm. Yet Andy Peyote was more of a kindred spirit to the
Farm children than he was to Chauncey and Bernsie. Mickey
Peyote and Stephen Gaskin and the people from the various
commune camps, married and unmarried, with or without leaders, have basically agreed on how children should behave. Their
notions and ours were so different that we began to see a counterculture personality emerging around that communal agreement. Not necessarily a tight political network like that John
Kimmey envisioned for the Taos valley; but a kind of spiritual
network of people who think and act in roughly the same way. If
a new kind of child is emerging from anyplace, it is from the
rural communes. Not from the political radicals and free school

families, where children were either lost in unworkable fantasies or else acted just like the kid next door. Not from the religious places, where the different style of life had little to do with a different kind of child. It was in the rural communes where we found something clear and definable and ultimately challenging about the new children.

Commune children, in general, were allowed a physical freedom that would make a city mother cringe. At each age group, they traveled beyond the limits of sanity. Little children were left alone at the Ranch with piles of old tools and dangerous objects. Seven- and eight-year-olds were left alone inside the domes at The Last Resort with sharp knives, stoves, and power saws. Teenagers were left alone at the Taos Learning Center with drugs and guns and sex; twelve-year-olds were left alone on the highway to thumb rides from strangers. Whatever hadn't happened to these children directly, they had probably seen happen to other people. Even at the Farm, where the children were allowed less direct freedom, they could watch their parents fucking. At other communes, the children witnessed drag-out brawls and marital fights, acid sessions and occasional orgies, epidemics and parental freak-outs of all kinds. There was no attempt on the part of parents to cushion or protect their children from physical danger or from heavy emotional experiences. When a couple was about to break up, they did not consult a psychiatrist or buy a book on how to tell the kid, or try to convey the news in a controlled or delicate way. Commune children did not receive censored news; they were there when the spaghetti hit the wall, when the shit hit the fan, when the baby was born. Their days were filled with uncontrollable happenings that are becoming rarer in the outside world—where parents lower their voices, where people die in hospitals, where sex happens behind closed doors, where death and sex are taught as high school courses instead of directly experienced.

On a superficial level, at least, commune children appeared to handle scary issues and physical freedom without much difficulty. We witnessed a lot of near misses, but no children were seriously hurt or maimed by other children. There were two stories of children having been killed in communes; one was hit by a truck near Taos, another drowned in a river near The Last Resort. A child's death was as shattering to a commune as it was to an individual family—at The Last Resort they built a little shrine in the woods where people often spent the night alone to remember the child. But commune children were not standing under the floodgate of horrors that mothers fear will be unloosed if they let their guard down on their children's safety. Commune mothers did not believe that a preoccupation with safety ultimately made things any safer.

The great emotional upheavals around communes hadn't damaged the children either, at least not in any recognizable way. Dr. Spock tells us that opening the bedroom door during sex can have a chilling effect on a child, who won't understand the passions and will confuse them with violence. Whether such fears come from Victorian prudery or an American adversion to uncontrolled experiences of any kind, they appeared, in the commune world, to be unfounded. The children seemed to have a fairly mature attitude about bodies and sex. Among young children, there was no poo-poo or doo-doo talk, people showered together and shit together without a great amount of fanfare. Chauncey and Bernsie went through a kind of poo-poo lull, abandoning their previous fascination with the matter until we returned to Miami. Then it all came back. With the older children, there was an absence of jokes and come-ons and sexual swagger that comes with puberty. In communes, we heard none of the sexual bragging that was so important in Ben's life. There had been a certain amount of sex talk in the urban communes, but it disappeared out in the country. The burning issues of our own curiosity—sex and drugs—were not the major issues. We were met by so much indifference when asking children about sex and girlfriends and lovers that we stopped asking. Sex and bodies, there for all to see, lost their magical, captivating powers in the minds of children.

The most important thing to commune parents is that their children be straight. Being straight has to do with relating to other people in a simple and direct way. All the children did that. In the many communes we visited, we saw no skirt-clutchers or thumb-suckers, no leg-biters or couch-hiders, no victims of stage fright, no children for whom parents gave the apology, "It takes them time to warm up to strangers." Ours was an admittedly random sampling, but when you don't see a skirt-clutcher or a thumb-sucker after six months with children, you begin to notice. Especially when your own child is a skirt-clutcher.

In large, milling groups of people, there was not enough space for people to be introverted. One could assume that a large, milling group of people would be a perfect forum for children of the other extreme—the back-talkers, cartwheelers, mimics, comedians, and attention-getters of all kinds. But that kind of self-conscious behavior was also discouraged in communes. The last blatant play for attention we saw was from Mark at the Cosmic Circle, where he did his yoga routine deliberately to impress us. At the rural places, children were simply not allowed to show off. The Ranch children could get away with a certain number of antics, especially during the afternoon when the grownup defenses were down, but most of their antics did not directly involve grownups. Andy Peyote was allowed to roam with a teen-age gang, but he was not allowed to *act* like a member of a teenage gang. Pete was told not to smoke grass at The Last Resort, not because grass was bad, but because Pete was acting like a punk when he smoked it. Never had we encountered parents who were so concerned about how their children came across to others, a concern that was carried to the Farm extreme where every smile, gesture, and remark was scrutinized.

Commune children were permitted physical freedoms that made us nervous, but they were subject to emotional restrictions that were hard for us to accept. It was just a question of where you lay down your concern. An urban mother might worry about what time her kid comes home, who his friends are, whether he is taking drugs on the sly, whether he has VD. Given the potential gravity of those issues, she might dismiss as silly a concern about whether her child talks in jive, whether he slouches, whether he looks her in the eye when he speaks. Commune parents approached things the other way around. They didn't care so much what their children did, as how they behaved while doing it. Knowing the exact physical whereabouts of their children was not a maximum requirement. The maximum requirement was knowing what their children were feeling. One hears about suburban parents who wonder whether their children are fucking around. They are afraid to just come out and ask, afraid of what the answer might be, afraid their children might not tell the truth. (Or perhaps afraid that their children will tell the truth.) So their worry is worked out on the level of signals like what time the car must be returned to the garage. Commune parents take a more direct approach. They know their kids are fucking around, are taking drugs from time to time; they can share these experiences with the children; they try to figure out how their kids handle things on a personal level.

Commune people brag about a lack of control in their lives; but ultimately, as parents, they may have more control than suburban parents. There are no organized activities, no band practices or ballet lessons for children, so the control has nothing to do with a tight schedule. There are no intimations of gentility, so control has nothing to do with how things look. There are no parietal rules, so control doesn't have to do with what freedoms children are allowed. But there is the control of a lot of grown-ups paying attention to kids on a certain emotional level, watching for evidence of immaturity.

The children were often rowdy and sometimes destructive, but there was very little a child could do to freak out his parents. Little Ernestos were not throwing blocks at television sets; parents did not seem involved in guilt games and power struggles with children. Ernesto, the radicals' child, was constantly stringing out his mother by testing her belief in freedom and the boundaries she drew for him. Jeep, a Ranch child of the same age, was independent of the freedom struggle because he had nobody to protest against. Jeep was expected to behave in a way that Ernesto was not.

The entire counterculture began as an exercise in protest and symbolic rage, but the rural commune people had left that kind of thinking behind. We understood more clearly what that change meant when Jerry Rubin visited the Ranch with us. Rubin had defined counterculture for a lot of people, and yet he was visibly uncomfortable in a hangout commune. It wasn't that people were unfriendly to him; they accepted him like any other visitor. But the Ranch people were simply not involved in the world of image-making, hyperbole, mental gymnastics, and self-consciousness that Rubin represented. He made a few attempts at conversation, but the connections were never established, and soon Jerry Rubin asked if there were a TV set in the house. There happened to be one in the far corner of a basement that the commune people hardly ever watched, but Rubin retreated to the TV and turned on to an interview with Spiro Agnew. It was obvious that Rubin was more comfortable in the presence of Spiro Agnew than in the presence of his former followers upstairs. Agnew and Rubin were partners in a world of attention-getting, role-playing, and complaining, that commune people had nothing to do with. They would not allow their children to come on like Jerry Rubin.

Straight behavior was more important to commune parents than preparing their children to achieve or to take accustomed places in society. At the Farm, they said they were against "praise and blame," which means that there is no reason to point out a kid for special praise, or for special blame, no reason that any one child should be singled out from the others. Children were not told how cute they were, how smart they were, how pretty their clothes looked, or how well they did their assigned work. It cut out a lot of the action that Chauncey and Bernsie were accustomed to relying on. Berns, in fact, gave her dresses away at the Ranch, in a generous flourish partially motivated by the fact that her dresses weren't getting her anywhere. She went naked. Chauncey, who was accustomed to wowing groups of adults by being clever, got enough blank responses so that he gave up the attempt and stayed outside with the other children.

For the first time we could understand this relationship between achievement and behavior, and the price we pay for preparing our children for success. Nobody asked the question,

"What will you be when you grow up?" and the absence of that concept simplified discipline to a remarkable extent. People did not worry about whether a little girl should be a fireman or a nurse, whether a little boy was free to be a dancer; the only important question was whether the little girl is being a bitch right now, or the little boy is being a brat right now. In Miami, Bernsie was repeatedly praised for her artwork, until she began to call herself "an artist." There was a time during our trip when Bernsie had done something bad, and Susan tried to scold her. "I can't listen to you now," Berns said, "I'm being an artist." That kind of escape was unavailable to children who were not recognized for being good at something.

Commune parents themselves did not hide behind social roles, which is why women's liberation was irrelevant to them. Commune women did not particularly identify with city women who are fighting to trade one role for another role; it was all seen as part of the same ego trip. Commune people did not consider themselves to be either housewives or insurance salesmen. They did their work, but they did not identify with their work in the same way that outsiders do. Thus, the debate over whether little Julie should be taught that she, too, can someday become President was rendered meaningless. There were no better or worse jobs in communes, and Julie should not consider herself to be anything more than just Julie. Everything was too personalized for people to feel superior or inferior about the roles they played.

I found it very difficult to live with people who did not accept my own professional identity; through my difficulties I could understand how much cultural baggage I carried that commune children did not have to carry. I tried to call myself a writer, but they wouldn't always let me get away with it. My desire for privacy was not accepted as a writer's prerogative; commune people saw it as evidence of an inability to get along with people. In several communes, I was forced out of the tent and into the fields, not because the work was so important, but because people sensed that I was hiding. And it was true; I was hiding. Many times I demanded a typewriter and a quiet place to work just because I couldn't stand dealing with so many people. In the outside world, I could get away with being standoffish and reclusive, because people accept that that's how writers behave. In the communes, professionalism was not an excuse for arrogance, or reclusiveness, or indifference. Commune children were not being prepared to be professionals; nothing was important enough to merit special privacy.

Having our own professional defenses shattered saved a lot of phone calls to Bettelheim, Kozol, Holt, and Spock. In the beginning, we had envisioned an entire chapter called "Raps with the Experts," a suitable hit title under which important people could present their theories on commune children. It didn't take long to see how ludicrous that idea had been, given the nature of communes.

Commune parents did not exert any intellectual control over their children. The mind was not an organ to be developed, it was an organ to be bypassed. Communes were completely anti-intellectual places, not only because the people did not read many books, but also because children were not logically trained. The younger children at the Ranch were never told the reasons for anything. They were expected to learn discipline merely as a reaction to feeling—the mother gets mad so the kid knows he has done something wrong. Nobody relied on logic as the outside, objective proof of why things should be a certain way. It was enough that a grownup was mad—the child was kicked out of the kitchen or the house; or, at the Farm, sent away from the "energy center." As the parent did not use a logical arsenal against a child, the children did not develop logical defenses in retaliation. Consequently, there was a lack of what we know as "back talk" because there was a lack of original talk. There was no meeting of minds. Susan sensed that clearly; she was disturbed, at times, at having lost some familiar link to Chauncey's brain.

The closeness that existed between commune parents and children had a different quality than what we were accustomed to. Perhaps because children were not expected to become anything, parents did not express pride in what their children had done. Perhaps because of the absence of logical thinking, children were not expected to "live up to" anything. One phrase we never heard in a commune was: "You know better than that." We had already developed in Chauncey and Bernsie a kind of Mythical You, some other little person who lives inside them and does everything right. The Mythical You is the person who knows better, the person who "should be ashamed," the person to whom we address our disappointments: "I am surprised at You." When Chauncey and Bernsie did not behave well, it was often not enough to simply correct them; we resorted to those perfect beings inside, and made Chauncey and Bernsie feel treasonous for not living up to them. The beginning of the development of a conscience, those Mythical Yous. But commune parents did not attempt to reach their children in the same way. Their approach to discipline was more behavioral: "You've done it, kid, now get out of here." At sloppier places like the Ranch, where parents did not present a united front, the discipline sometimes broke down. At organized places like the Farm, where everybody pushed in the same direction, the discipline never collapsed. But in none of the communes did one find the bargaining with logic, morality, and guilt that often occurs in clashes between parents and children.

Perhaps for this reason, the commune approach to raising children limited much of the wrenching tug-of-war of the nuclear family. There was a kind of continuum at work—in urban communes the children were aware of their mothers' emotional incursions; in rural communes these incursions were mostly stamped out. The rural parents were not preoccupied with their children, with their health, their intelligence, their morality, in that familiar intense way. Some of the teenage girls at the Taos Learning Center had moved there to escape that kind of intensity at home. We met no resentful teenagers in communes. On those rare occasions in which fathers and sons were together, they were together in a beautiful communion. Andy and Mickey Peyote were like that; so was John Kimmey and his son Shawn. Like two friends, who could experience things equally, without a hint of that stern, reproachful edge of the father, or the struggle of the boy against his father's power.

Responsibility for children and their behavior was shared by the larger group, which usually took pressure off the parents (except at places like the Ranch where parents could never quite unite). Children found it more difficult to hide behind parents, or to be easily bailed out by them. Parents were not a point of reliance on that level—Andy Peyote never knew whether or not he would be allowed to stay in his father's dome. If Andy was being an asshole, somebody else at The Resort could have told him to leave for a few days—just what Mickey had told Pete. Andy knew that if he did something like throw a rock through Carl's dome, then he would have to work that out with Carl. It wouldn't have been any of Mickey's business; Mickey only cared when Andy was being weird in relation to him. Carl might talk to Andy, or deck him, and it wouldn't be any of Mickey's business. It was like that in most communes; from an early age kids learned that they had to get themselves out of trouble. In the urban communes, there was still a lingering sense that kids could step back behind mother if the going got heavy, but out in the rural places, it was strictly one-to-one.

There seemed to be no limit to how far communal responsibility could go. There was a commune called AAA, a teepee enclave occupied by a rock band and some women and kids. Ten women and one man had set aside a day to talk about their kids, reminiscent of the Cosmic Circle meetings, except without a lot of psychological jostling and uneasiness. On this particular day, they were talking about Jonah, a four-year-old retarded child. Jonah apparently would not cooperate with his mother and wasn't completely toilet-trained. He was a slow learner and often demanded extra care. In effect, he was a problem, a drag on the community. The people discussed him with such loving familiarity, though, that it was impossible to tell, after thirty minutes, which was the actual mother of Jonah. You somehow felt that every child at AAA was the equal concern of every mother.

It was interesting to see how a commune handled a retarded child, a severe problem for a nuclear, urban family. It is the kind of problem that leads a nuclear family to seek professional help—perhaps a special school or even a specialized home to deal with the child's disability. At the AAA, the mothers discussed sending Jonah to a home in Denver, but they rejected the idea as evidence of a lack of responsibility, and a lack of love. Experts were viewed as a poor substitute for friends.

As the discussion progressed, you could sense that love was actually beginning to work in Jonah's favor. Jonah wasn't there at the time, but love altered the way they were talking about it. It started out on the level of his problems, his retardation, the pain in the ass that Jonah was to take care of. But then Sylvia, a woman who moved here from the Farm and still sounded exactly like Gaskin, suggested that Jonah also gave something good to the community. She said he was a superior person in certain areas, especially his sensitivity; that he was like a person on an acid trip who may find the world unbelievably beautiful one minute and ugly and scary the next. Everybody had taken acid at the AAA; they knew what she was talking about, it seemed like a breakthrough idea. If we can treat him like he is on acid, she said, then we will get along with him better. Sylvia managed to make her vision of Jonah so specific that she turned his retardation into something positive without sounding patronizing like a spokesman for Easter Seals or Olympics for the crippled. The rest of the group picked up on it, and began to discuss the things Jonah had done or said that were important. They projected into the future, what jobs in the community he could handle as an adult, and decided there was plenty at a farm that a retarded person could do.

Finally, they pinpointed the other problem, which was Jonah's mother June. Sylvia said that June let Jonah rip her off, a lot of his retardation was just "clever stoned rip-off behavior" because Jonah knew he would be coddled. Sylvia said June shouldn't let Jonah get away with that. June was relieved to hear that; she knew Jonah made her feel uncomfortable at times, but she didn't know why. It would have sounded cruel for her to suggest that the poor retarded kid was just playing on her pity. But it was useful for Sylvia to suggest it. The rest of the mothers said they would put some pressure on Jonah not to play on his handicap, and there the discussion ended.

Communes could absorb a lot. Not only constant visitors and occasional runaway children, but retarded people and old people and other kinds of people who are seen as problems in the outside world. The Farm was advertising for old people to move in, to round out the generations—not as a gesture of nobility, but because Stephen Gaskin thought old people to be an indispensable part of a family. The Farm was also advertising for babies that outsider mothers did not want. Other communes were not that deliberate in their requests, but all of them could handle a lot of people. It seemed as if communes were expanding their responsibility, their sense of how much they could take, while the nuclear family is further restricting itself. Communes take on more children, more dogs, more relatives, more disruptions, while the nuclear family reduces its size, sends grandmother to the old-age home, little Billy to the rehabilitation center, Sally to a northern college, parceling off its people according to the needs of a more professional society. If our children don't leave home to become specialists, then they leave home to be treated by them.

For all the superficial chaos, the commune children live in a simpler, more protected environment. They know who makes decisions in the community, and how those decisions can be affected. They can trace each element of their life to the source—where the water comes from, where the food comes from. Their behavior, and what is expected of them, is not confused by impersonal issues like children's rights and children's future roles in society. They are spared any involvement with salesmen, with television, with government agencies, with disc jockeys hyped on forty cups of coffee. To Gaskin this is the most important protection a commune provides, a kind of moat around the subconscious that cuts off the paranoid and hostile vibes of the outside world. There is sometimes trouble inside communes, but children are not affected by the random influences of city life: teachers, television, doctors, experts. When there are troubles, or troubled people, the communes can muster a collective force to deal with them. And they have eliminated a lot of the built-in trouble of people making money from each other. We rarely saw a monetary transaction in a commune.

So you have the paradox of children who are not individually spared from death, sex, freak-outs, or pain, living in a world that collectively protects them from the bad vibes of America. The Farm was the extreme of protection, of course; we couldn't imagine a Farm kid spending five minutes on a city playground without being totally unraveled. Gaskin says they won't have to go to a city playground because the Farm will survive, and why should he teach his children to be hostile and aggressive and paranoid? But even in the less permanent communes, the children were tied to the group; they seemed lost without it. Sometimes we worried about the Ranch children, their lack of self-definition, their total reliance on the pack. But then there was Taos, and The Last Resort, and older children like Andy, who was more self-reliant and independent than any child we knew. Andy and his Castaneda outlook and his sense of security that came from a much less frail source than the security of bank accounts and insurance policies and good grades and seat belts. Would the Ranch children develop into Andy Peyotes? Did the network of communes, and the movement between them, create that sense of independence? We didn't know.

It was hard to know what commune children would end up doing. In the world around communes, there are few assurances. Nobody talks about the future, and except in the religious communities, nobody claims to know. There are calamities and twists of fate. People are arrested. Communes are torn down, people quarantined, schools abolished, plans scuttled, relationships crumble, and projects are dissolved on a daily basis. Trying to hold on to any of this is looked on as a bad trip—creating that kind of security, Mickey Peyote says, is creating fear.

The aim of commune life is to be high. The children are being prepared, not to get into college, but to feel good. Gaskin believed in being high without drugs, and his commune lived by that belief. When we began our book, we worried about the effects of artificial drugs on children (and we saw no bad effects), but it became clear that the commune is itself a kind of drug. The stoned state, they call it—to get into the stoned state you have to feel good about yourself and what you are doing. You have to deal with other people in a loving way. Everybody is in the stoned state from time to time, whatever word they use to describe that kind of exhilaration. But Gaskin is right; the longer we stayed in communes, the more timeless, orderless days we went through, the more easily we could enter that state of wandering and not worrying. Questions like "Will the communal movement survive?" are outsider's questions, questions from another culture. When you are in a commune, questions like that tend to disappear, they have nothing to do with trying to live the moment. Andy Peyote saw his life as a "trip," a trip in a more primeval world of no appointments and no assurances. When we plugged into that trip, then we could understand what it meant to be a commune child. A child of a marginal civilization who learns that getting through the day is the most important thing, and that you have to be very uptight to build a city or a pyramid.

One of our original preoccupations was whether commune children could get back into the regular stream of things. There is a confusion in the American mind about choices, about the choices that our children enjoy. An American child is expected to be able to do that: change his life, change his career, change his scene. A child who grows up an Auca Indian has to be an Auca Indian forever, but an American child can start out as a surfer and still have a chance to be President. It is the difference, we say, between a free culture and an imprisoning culture.

But being in communes taught us of the imprisonment of our own culture. We wanted to think of alternative lifestyles as part of the American dream, just another choice that people could step into, or step out of. But you cannot just step into a commune. Communes involve a revolution in behavior, a revolution in how children are allowed to act. Americans don't usually think of their choices as having anything to do with their character. Dr. Spock tells us that certain behavior is just natural in all children, part of the genetic pool that will bubble up no matter whatever a parent does.

Maybe all American children do behave in a universal, natural way, but that is because we have trained them to do that. At several points in our trip we would look at a commune child and say, "Just a little kid, running around, like all other kids, and what's the sense of writing about him?" But then we would return to visit a friend in some straight community and be reminded of what it really means to be a commune child. There was a married couple in San Francisco, a liberal lawyer and his wife, and daughter named Jeanette. Jeanette was Bernsie's age. Our first contact with her was when she was guarding the door to her upstairs bedroom, throwing all her toys in the closet so Bernsie couldn't play with them. It took her two days to say hello to us. ("Don't worry," Jeanette's mother said, "it takes time for little girls to warm up.") It took her three days to warm up to Bernsie, three days of temper tantrums and hair-pulling incidents and telling on each other to their mommies and tussling over dolls. Bernsie fell right back into that kind of competitiveness; it was in the air.

Chauncey immediately wanted to make friends with a neighborhood boy who lived across the street. Our friends told him not to cross the street, and sounded definitely discouraging. We said it was OK for Chauncey to cross by himself, he knew about cars, and then they gave us the real reason for their reluctance: "Don't let Chauncey go over there," our friends said, "we think our neighbor is a child molester." "A child molester? Have you talked to the neighbor, have you talked to anybody about it?" "No, we don't like to mention it. We're not sure."

Here we were on a city block of nuances and paranoia, unsureness about neighbors but no way to work it out, and separate children guarding their separate doors. Jeanette, a four-year-old, already took two different kinds of art lessons, and had her work plastered on the walls, and called herself an artist—and was a complete bitch, in the commune perspective. Her mother was vaguely dissatisfied with Jeanette's arrogance and temper tantrums, but she didn't know anything could be done about them. Another guilty mother.

There was nothing in Dr. Spock that would cover both Jeanette and Jeep, or Jeanette and a Farm child of the same age. And there is a price to be paid on both sides. Commune parents wanted a kind of emotional goodness for their children—which they gave them at the cost of the self-centered drive that leads to great personal achievement. We couldn't see famous writers or scientists coming out of that generation of ragamuffins. We still had that self-centered drive, that urge for private fantasy and mental exercise, enough so that we could not continue to live in a commune. But we could no longer believe that Chauncey and Bernsie were superior to commune children. We could not hand our egos and our minds down to Chauncey and Bernsie without handing them a lot of that attendant ugliness that communes had stamped out.

R4